A Centennial Exhibition

September 19 | November 30

1 9 9 7

THE FELLOWSHIP OF THE PENNSYLVANIA ACADEMY OF THE FINE ARTS

The Unbroken Line

1897~1997

PUBLISHED BY

The Fellowship
An Alumni Association of the
Pennsylvania Academy of the Fine Arts
Philadelphia, Pennsylvania

Pennsylvania Academy of the Fine Arts Fellowship's Centennial Contributors

Benefactors

Mrs. Beatrice Pitcairn
Mrs. Dorrance H. Hamilton
Mrs. Jane Cox MacElree

Patrons

Mr. & Mrs. Benjamin Alexander
Mr. & Mrs. Charles L. Andes
The Annenberg Foundation
Felicity R.S. Benoliel
Mr. & Mrs. Theodore W. Brickman, Jr.
Mr. & Mrs. Donald R. Caldwell
Mrs. Judith Mandell Delfiner
Mrs. Betty N. Gordon
Mr. & Mrs. John C. Haas
Mrs. Lorna U. Hauslohner
Mr. & Mrs. Kenneth F. Herlihy
Mr. & Mrs. George B. Lemmon, Sr.
Mr. & Mrs. Howard H. Lewis
Mr. & Mrs. Sam S. McKeel
Mrs. J. Maxwell Moran
Ms. Naomi Pitcairn
Pitcairn Trust Company
Mr. & Mrs. Meyer P. Potamkin
William C. & Catherine Rieser
Ms. Barbara Walley Schaff
Regina Bannan & Allen Serody
Mr. & Mrs. James M. Stewart
Mrs. Harriette S. Tabas

The artists in this catalogue may be reached by contacting the Fellowship Office at (215) 972-7600 ext. 3507.

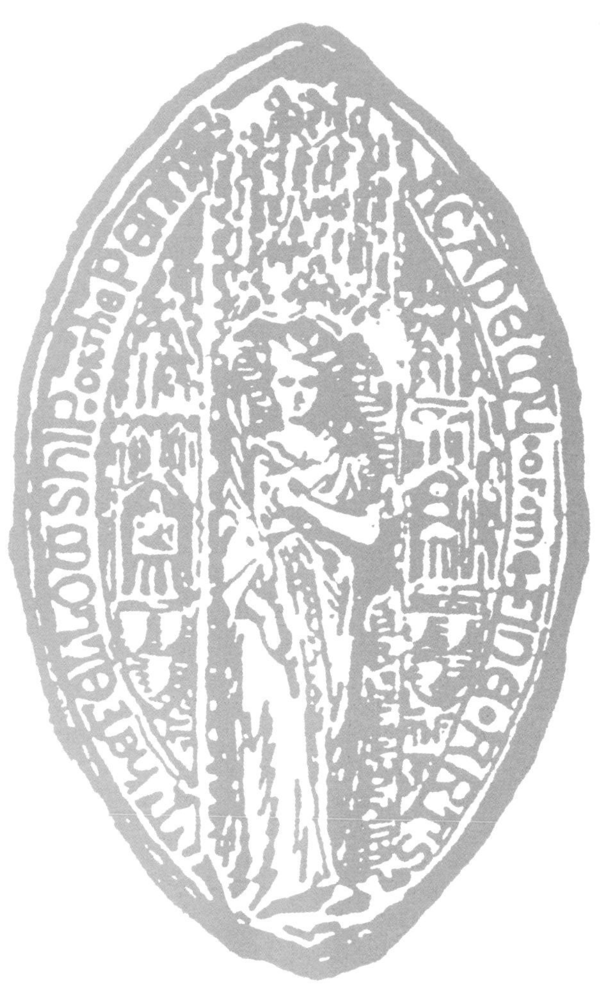

Above: Original Seal of the Fellowship, c.1901

Pages 3 & 12
background images: Casts from a 1901 Academy School Drawing Class

Library of Congress Catalog Number: 97-61391

ISBN: 0-9659340-0-4

Catalogue: Barbara Sosson Design

. . . and now for the next hundred years.

Rodger LaPelle, *President*
Fellowship of the Pennsylvania Academy
of the Fine Arts

✧ ✧ ✧

*T*his year, 1997, is a special year for the Fellowship of the Pennsylvania Academy of the Fine Arts. It is "The Centennial Year" — one hundred years of "Artists Helping Artists," which defines the Fellowship.

For this important occasion, the Annual Juried Exhibition is taking place in the Museum of American Art of the Pennsylvania Academy of the Fine Arts. After ten years, we are finally exhibiting at home. Thank you, Gresham Riley, Academy President, for this opportunity.

My involvement as Chairperson of the Centennial Events has given me an even greater admiration of the nobility of all the artists in this wonderful, independent organization — an Alumni organization of the Pennsylvania Academy of the Fine Arts — the Fellowship. As we know, artists must be free to create, free to be independent, free to choose, and to not be categorized, and so must the Fellowship. The natural energy of its artists is the strength upon which the Fellowship survives. Let us continue to grow in this aura of freedom.

I want to express my deepest gratitude and appreciation to the Fellowship's friend and Dean of the School, Frederick Osborne; Rodger LaPelle, our President; Garth Herrick and Susan Land, my co-chairpersons; and to Betty Zeleznik, my secretary. Their assistance and that of the many Fellowship volunteers who gave their time and efforts have made this Centennial year, and especially this exhibition, a memorable success.

Happy 100th Birthday to the Fellowship of the Pennsylvania Academy of the Fine Arts!!!

Ruth C. Davis,
Executive Vice President and
Chairperson of the Centennial Events
July 4, 1997

*T*he Pennsylvania Academy of the Fine Arts was ninety-two years old, and had several thousand alumni, when the Fellowship was founded in 1897. The first task this group addressed was identifying opportunities for its members to exhibit their work. The Annual Juried Exhibition became its single greatest effort to publicly promote the talents of its constituency, and has become the trademark of the organization.

As the trustees, faculty, students, and staff of the Pennsylvania Academy of the Fine Arts celebrate the Fellowship's Centennial, we reflect with pride on one-hundred years of this organization's dedication to service — service to the fine arts, to the Academy, and, most of all, to Academy artists.

There are countless stories of "artists helping artists." While the details differ, the common thread is the Fellowship helping Academy artists — financially, spiritually, technically, and professionally.

This year's celebratory edition of the Fellowship exhibition features one-hundred-and-forty-four juried works. It suitably demonstrates the extraordinary diversity of artistic thinking, and commitment to excellence, that becomes indigenous to those who study at the Academy.

It is appropriate that the Fellowship's Centennial be commemorated as this year's premier exhibition in the Academy's Museum of American Art, and that the occasion be enhanced from the Museum's own resources. The galleries adjoining the Juried Annual are hung with an extensive survey of historical works from the Museum's permanent collection by graduates and former students, including a focus on Violet Oakley, an officer and prominent member of the Fellowship for fifty years, and recipient of its Gold Medal of Honor. In addition, there are profiles of five living alumni — Vincent Desiderio, David Lynch, Jody Pinto, Raymond Saunders, and Sidney Simon — who have received distinguished recognition in the contemporary art world.

In a tribute to its spirit, the Fellowship has selected Sam Maitin, an artist who did not graduate from the Academy but who espouses all those qualities that the Academy stands for, to receive its prestigious Percy M. Owens Memorial Award. Similarly, the organization has marked its hundredth year by creating a new Award for Lifetime Artistic Achievement, bestowing the first citation on Ben Kamihira, who received the Percy M. Owens Memorial Award in 1966.

The Academy is very pleased to have this opportunity to express its appreciation to this organization that for one-hundred years has unfailingly stewarded the mission and great traditions of this institution.

Frederick S. Osborne
Dean and Director of the School
July 1997

Chester Springs class,
c. 1920

Acknowledgments

We thank . . .

all the artists whose contributions made this publication a reality

all of our friends and patrons who gave support and help

the Pennsylvania Academy of the Fine Arts — our host for *The Unbroken Line 1897-1997*, the Annual Juried Exhibition for the 100th Anniversary of the Fellowship of the Pennsylvania Academy of the Fine Arts and the entire staff of the Pennsylvania Academy of the Fine Arts

Dr. Gresham Riley
President of the Pennsylvania Academy of the Fine Arts

Dr. Frederick S. Osborne, Jr.
Dean/Director of the School, Pennsylvania Academy of the Fine Arts

Ruth C. Davis
Centennial Events Chairperson

Susan Land
Centennial Events Co-Chairperson

Garth Herrick
Centennial Events Co-Chairperson

Rodger LaPelle
President of the Fellowship of the Pennsylvania Academy of the Fine Arts

Jurors for *The Unbroken Line 1897-1997, 100 Years of Fellowship: A Centennial Exhibition*
Luis Cruz Azaceta, *Painter, New Orleans, La.*
Philip Pearlstein, *Painter, New York, N.Y.*
Sylvia Yount, *Curator, Museum of American Art of the Pennsylvania Academy of the Fine Arts, Philadelphia, Pa.*

all of the Fellowship artists who participated in the Centennial Events

Lindsay Brinton, Chester Springs Studio, Chester Springs, Pa. and Sandra Momyer and Dr. Priscilla Waggoner, Historic Yellow Springs, Inc., Chester Springs, Pa.
Hosts for our Reunion and Homecoming Picnic

Kate Brockman
Sculptor, design and execution of "The Fellow" for our Hall of Fame

Lillian Danziger and Fred Danziger
Calligraphers of award and prize certificates

Susan James-Gadzinski
Editorial assistance

Tom M. Jackson and Eileen W. Jackson
Artists' statement coordinators

Susan Land
Calligraphy for Centennial Celebration launching party

Cheryl Liebold
Archivist, the Pennsylvania Academy of the Fine Arts

Beatrice Pitcairn
Hostess for our Centennial Celebration launching party

Restaurant School
Centennial birthday cake

Barbara Sosson Design
Centennial Graphic image and Exhibition catalogue design and production

Miriam Seidel
Catalogue essay

Jeffrey Ware, Dock Street Brewery
Beverages for the Masked Ball

Elizabeth Zeleznik
Centennial Events Secretary

the catalogue photographers...

Artist / Photographer(s)

Lorraine Alexander/Karen Mauch
Eleanor Allen/Rick Echelmeyer
Dennis Aufiery/Matt Wargo
Bethany Anne Ayres/Michael Sarnaki
Frank Bender/Frank Bender
Philip J. Carroll/Ken Hohing
Nancy Citrino/Marty Fumo
Beth Lea Clardy/Wharton Photography
Jacqueline Cotter/Joe Painter
Deborah Deichler/Rick Echelmeyer
Margaretta Gilboy/Joe Painter
Barbara Goodstein/D. James Dee
Christopher Hornbeck/Will Brown
Hei Myung C. Hyun/Scott Lindgren
Nancy M. Jaramillo/David Croby and Vanessa Rood
Richard J. Johnson/Karen Mauch
Tom King/Joe Painter
John C. Kline/Karen Mauch
Rita Klinger/Karen Mauch
Elaine M. Lisle/Karen Mauch
Sam Maitin/Will Brown
Lydia Martin/Lars Nordin
Elizabeth Meyer/Karen Mauch
Ellen Miller/Professional Color
Johanna M. Petropoulos/Karen Mauch
Douglas W. Randall/Asterick, Inc.
David Shevlino/Joe Painter
Jim Simmons/John Manning
Joy Smith/Pat Daley
Rebecca Dvorin Strong/Charles Backus
Mayumi Tomii/Joe Painter
Elizabeth Wilson/Tom Marr
Harriet Zeitlin/Brian Forrest

Photographs throughout the text are courtesy of the Archives of the Pennsylvania Academy of the Fine Arts; Scholarship Voyage photo courtesy of the Cunard Steamship Co., Ltd. Photographs of Felicity R.S. Benoliel and Linda Lee Alter by Joseph Routon

A Century of Fellowship:

The Fellowship of the Pennsylvania Academy of the Fine Arts' First One Hundred Years

On the evening of April 19, 1897, five hundred students and former students packed the Lecture Room of the Pennsylvania Academy of the Fine Arts. They had come in response to an invitation prepared by the Academy's Managing Director, Harrison S. Morris, and President, Edward H. Coates, and signed by 32 prominent artists, to participate in "the formation of an Alumni Fellowship of the Academy Schools." The Academy itself was by this time ninety-two years old.

Within weeks the new organization adopted a name: "The Fellowship of the Pennsylvania Academy of the Fine Arts"; and a mission: "to foster a spirit of fraternity among students of the Pennsylvania Academy of the Fine Arts in the interests of Art." "Any person who has been or who is a student" of the Academy would be eligible for membership.

The first Board and Officers of the Fellowship included a number of distinguished artists: Henry Thouron, Cecilia Beaux, Thomas Anshutz, Emily Sartain, Colin Campbell Cooper, Hugh Breckenridge, and John Sloan. Charles Dana became the Fellowship's first President. Among his first motions was a proposal to establish a Fellowship Prize to be awarded at the Academy's Annual Exhibition. The first Fellowship Prizes, of $15 and $10, were actually awarded at the annual Student Exhibition of 1900.

This early action encapsulated two of the Fellowship's interlinked goals, as they would develop over the years: to help other artists and to encourage them in their artistic endeavors. In addition, the Fellowship found its identity in involvement with larger social issues as they affected artists, and in fostering "a spirit of fraternity" through lectures, events, and sundry entertainments.

By 1922, the Fellowship celebrated its 25th Anniversary as a solid organization

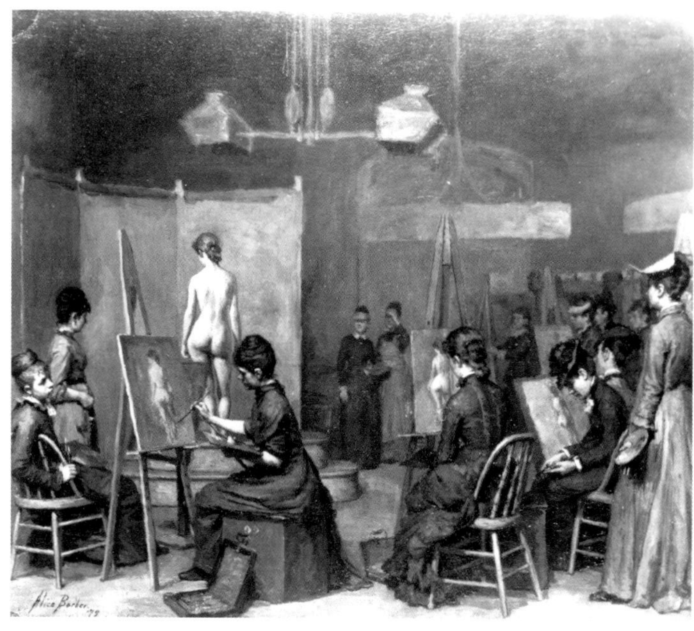

Alice Barber Stephens, *The Women's Life Class*, c. 1879, oil on cardboard (grisaille), 12 x 14" Collection of the Museum of American Art of the Pennsylvania Academy of the Fine Arts

with a high profile on Philadelphia's cultural scene. That year the Fellowship's own Annual Exhibition, its tenth, had opened at the Art Alliance. Over 400 revelers attended its silver anniversary party, an Alice in Wonderland-themed evening of pageant, music, and dance. The procession following Fellowship President Mary Butler and Academy President John Frederick Lewis into the hall included Hugh Breckenridge as the Mad Hatter, Alice Kent Stoddard as the Cook, Frank Reed Whiteside as the White Knight, and Violet Oakley as the Queen of Hearts.[1] "The Academy Fling," an original work for six musicians, opened the dance. This extravagant affair was not the only Fellowship social event that year; others included a "Deep Sea Ball," and the Annual Outing, with supper in the woods, at the studio of Joseph T. Pearson.

The Fellowship's more strictly art-oriented activities that year showed in other ways how far the group had developed. In addition to its Annual, numerous smaller exhibits were mounted at 1834 Arch Street, the Fellowship's meeting place at the time; and at several clubs, public schools, a settlement house, and a factory. The Picture Purchase Fund, begun by Mary Butler in 1912, had

[1] Twenty-fifth Annual Report of the Fellowship, Philadelphia, 1922. A member of the Fellowship for over fifty years, Violet Oakley received a special award from the Fellowship in 1955, on the Academy's 150th Anniversary.

already begun acquiring work from artists, building up a permanent collection for the Fellowship.

While these activities — social fellowship, exhibitions, and encouragement of artists — have been a continuing hallmark of the Fellowship up to the present, they do not characterize the work of a typical alumni association. Why is this? The Fellowship was born at a time of extraordinary enthusiasm for cultural fellowship, in Philadelphia and the country. The 1890's saw the foundation of a number of local cultural associations: the Pen and Pencil Club (1892, now the oldest continuously operating press club in the nation); the Philobiblon Club, a literary society (1893); the Plastic Club, a still-operating organization for women artists (1897); and the Graphic Sketch Club, later to become Fleisher Art Memorial (1898).[2]

Yet, even compared with other art school alumni groups founded around the same time, like that of the Philadelphia School of Design for Women (now Moore College of Art and Design), which held annual exhibitions in the early part of this century, the Fellowship's mission was unusually focused on providing support and professional encouragement to its members. An alum of the Academy, one of only a few institutions devoted to the fine arts in this country — then or now — possessed career goals and professional needs different from graduates of other schools, even from those of more trade-oriented art schools. The Fellowship aimed from the start to meet those needs.

Exhibitions

One steadfast aspect of the Fellowship's mission has been to provide exhibition opportunities for its members. Its first exhibition, devoted to sketches (a daring concept then), debuted to great interest in the Academy's galleries in 1901. The first of its Annual Exhibitions was hung in May 1912, at the Plastic Club (many of whose members also belonged to the Fellowship). In addition to its Annuals, through the 1930's the

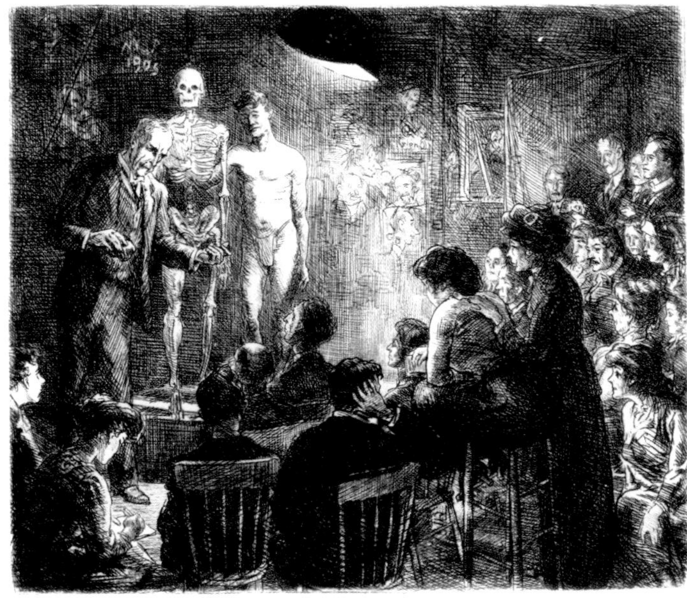

John Sloan, *Anshutz on Anatomy,* 1912 etching, 7 1/2 x 9" Collection of the Museum of American Art of the Pennsylvania Academy of the Fine Arts

[2] Jean Barth Toll and Mildred S. Gillam, eds., *Invisible Philadelphia* (Philadelphia: Atwater Kent Museum, 1995), pp. 975-83, 1038, 1086.

Fellowship would follow an ambitious program of satellite exhibits in other cities — a 1923 exhibition in Atlantic City was estimated to have been visited by 300,000 people! — as well as in Philadelphia public schools, libraries, and other institutions.

Also through the thirties, the Fellowship Annual remained a pilgrim, travelling to various art venues: the Plastic Club and the Philadelphia Sketch Club (often hosting in tandem), the Art Alliance (from 1919 through 1923), the Art Club, and the New Century Club, among others. In 1940, the Fellowship was invited to hold its Annual Exhibition in the Pennsylvania Academy of the Fine Arts' Museum Galleries for the first time. This arrangement continued for nearly three decades. In 1969, the Academy ended its own Annual Exhibition, and at the same time ceased hosting the Fellowship Annual; the Fellowship would not exhibit in the Academy Museum again until 1987.

Since 1969, the Fellowship Annual Exhibition has resumed its travelling; that year it showed at the Philadelphia Civic Center. The Annual's venues since 1984 have included: the Rodger LaPelle Gallery (1984), the Peale House Galleries of the Academy (1985), the Noyes Museum (1986), the Academy Museum, for its 90th Anniversary Annual (1987), the Port of History Museum (1988), the American College (1989, 1994), the James A.

Michener Art Museum (1990), the Woodmere Art Museum (1991, 1993, 1996), the Philip and Muriel Berman Museum (1992), and West Chester University's McKinney Gallery (1995).

Education and Entertainment

From its first meetings, the Fellowship endeavored to offer lectures and other educational programs for its members. William Merritt Chase gave many lectures, on Velázquez (1899), Whistler (whom he had known, 1905), and other topics, to packed audiences. Henry Mercer spoke on his methods of reproducing early tile-making processes (1902 and 1905), and in 1916 Cecilia Beaux spoke on "What American Artists Owe to France." Numerous other lecturers reported on contemporary art developments, art processes, and members' travels. In 1957, the invited lecturers included architect Louis Kahn, Marcel Duchamp, and Robert Motherwell.

Fellowship fêtes tended to be exuberantly creative, starting with the first ball, held in 1898, on the theme of Shakespeare, with reenactments from Julius Caesar. Others took the themes of Robin Hood (1899), a "May-Pole Party" (1901), and "A Night on Mars" (1919). In 1930, with the advent of the Depression, a "Hard Times" party was held, with the aim of benefiting the Picture Purchase Fund. That same year, modern dance pioneers Doris Humphrey and Charles Weidman offered a "Modern Classic Dance Demonstration" in the Lecture Hall. In the 1940's, Chinese Dinners were held yearly in Chinatown; 100 attended the 1946 Dinner, which included a lecture on current Chinese art.

Each spring, continuing for many decades up through the 1950's, members enjoyed an Annual Outing picnic, at such scenic locations as the Morris Arboretum, Chester Springs, or the homes of Violet Oakley, Joseph T. Pearson, and John Frederick Lewis. Since 1977, the Fellowship Picnic has been held yearly at Saunders Woods, the Hatfield House, and other locations.

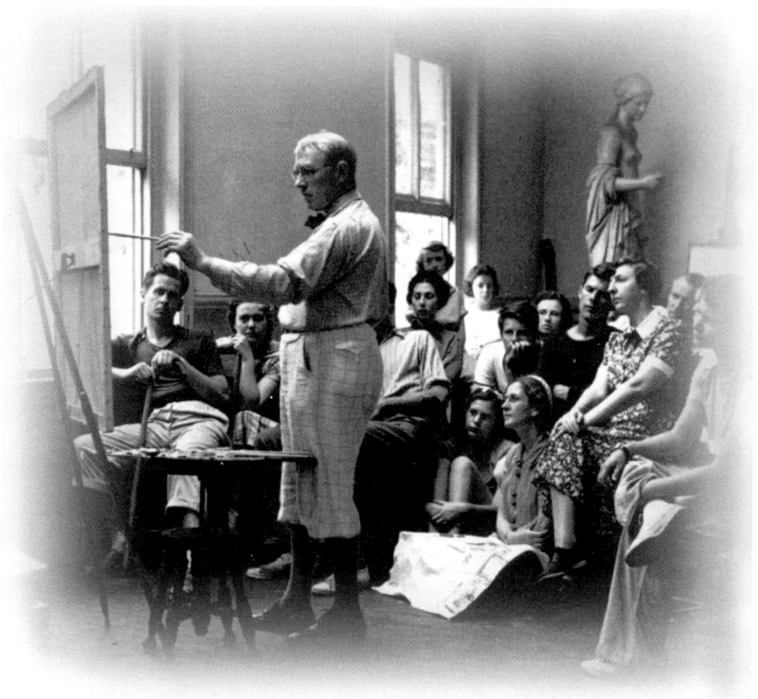

Daniel Garber in class at Chester Springs, 1930's

A continuing issue has been the Fellowship's need for a home base for meetings, exhibitions, and events. Beginning in the Academy's Print Room, the Fellowship moved in 1905 to quarters at 201 South 11th Street, then back to the Academy in 1911. This back-and-forth movement has continued to the present. Most recently, the Hatfield House, a historic building in Fairmount Park, was home to the Fellowship from 1989 to 1994 Since then, the Fellowship has again maintained an office and held meetings in the Academy.

Aid to Artists and Social Action

From its early years, the Fellowship saw itself as representing its constituency in the world of larger issues. The Fellowship made its voice heard on the issue of employment for artists during the W.P.A. years, joined in an anti-billboard campaign, and protested the judging of artists' work by government agencies in the early 1960's.

During the two World Wars, Fellowship members acted to support the war effort. In 1918, several benefit events raised over $3,000. This was donated to the Red Cross for the purchase of five ambulances, to be named in honor of Henry J. Thouron, Thomas Eakins, Thomas P. Anshutz, William

M. Chase, and General Pershing. During World War II, the Fellowship sponsored classes in camouflage painting.

The Fellowship's mission to provide direct aid and support to artists may lie at the heart of its identity. From the first Fellowship Prize, it has demonstrated a commitment to directly benefiting artists which has grown over the years. The evolution of Fellowship philanthropy bears the stamp of one person, Mary Butler, President from 1920 to 1937, but actively involved in the Fellowship from 1909 until her death in 1946 at age 81. The daughter of iron magnate James Butler, she early devoted herself to a life in art, but found her second calling in helping other artists.

Butler was instrumental in initiating the Fellowship's first fund, the Picture Purchase Fund, in 1913 (it later became the Mary Butler Memorial Fund). Funds were used to buy art from members, providing them recognition and financial reward, and creating a permanent collection for the Fellowship. The Henry J. Thouron Fund, initiated by a bequest from the Fellowship's second president, and fully endowed through Butler's efforts by 1925, offers interest-free loans to Fellowship artists in times of financial emergency. For many decades, the Thouron Fund also paid artists to teach art in local settlement houses.

By the early 1980's, both the Thouron and Butler Funds had fallen dormant; their trust accounts were referred to Orphan's Court for disposition. Research by Fellowship Board members was able to demonstrate their original purpose, and both accounts were reopened and returned to the Fellowship. In addition, the Fellowship's collection of several hundred artworks, acquired through the 1930's by the Picture Purchase Fund, was sold at auction by Christie's, between 1985 and 1987. The considerable appreciation of some works over a half-century allowed the Mary Butler Fund to renew substantial, regular purchases of work from Fellowship artists. A new policy allows for constant

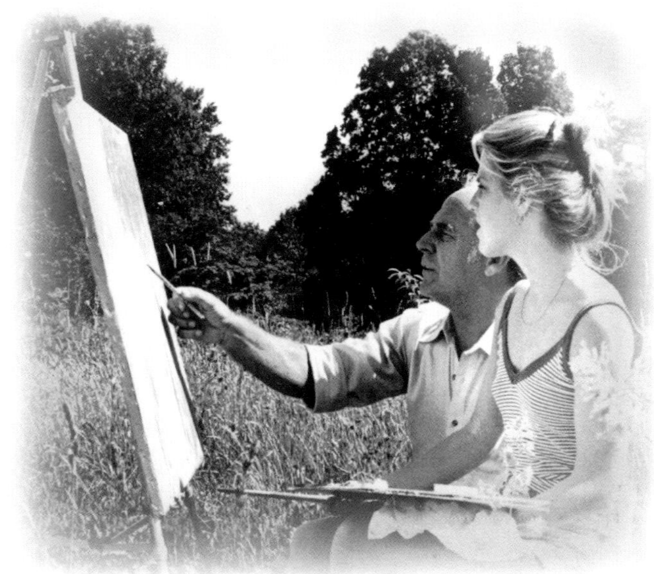

Jimmy C. Lueders teaching a landscape class

sales from the collection, to replenish its purchasing power.

Over the years, many special prizes and awards have been created to be presented during the Fellowship Annual Exhibition. These now number more than thirty, including the Percy M. Owens Memorial Award, presented each year to a distinguished Pennsylvania Artist. This year a new Fellowship award, for Lifetime Artistic Achievement, will be awarded in the form of an artist-designed bronze trophy. The first recipient will be Ben Kamihira, longtime Fellowship member and instructor at the Academy.

The Fellowship enters its second century with an active membership of over 600 and a vigorous Board committed to continuing the Fellowship's history of acting in support of its community of artists, fostering that spirit of fraternity felt among those who have benefited from the special environment of the Pennsylvania Academy of the Fine Arts.

Miriam Seidel

Many thanks to Quita Brodhead, Fred Danziger, Ruth C. Davis, Bette Lawler Greenwood, William J. Greenwood, Garth Herrick, Sophia Hewryk, Rodger LaPelle, Cheryl Leibold, Frederick S. Osborne, and Barbara Sosson for their assistance in the preparation of this essay.

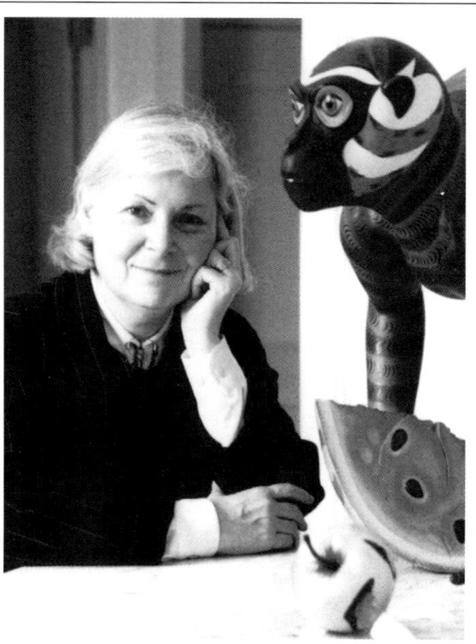

Linda Lee Alter

The happiest times of my childhood were spent watching my grandmother, Bessie Berman, design and sew clothing for herself, her daughters, and her grandchildren. As I have grown older, my memory of that joy has deepened into a great respect both for her art and her generosity.

For almost thirty years, before turning to painting, I created fabric appliqué wall hangings from the coat, suit, and dress fabrics Grandmom taught me to love. In 1993, I realized my long desire to "give back" to my community by founding The Leeway Foundation. A private charitable foundation, Leeway is dedicated to encouraging and supporting Philadelphia's many outstanding women artists.

Leeway awards grants for excellence annually to individual women artists, 25 years or older, who have resided in the five-county Philadelphia area for at least two years. Each year grants are made in a different arts discipline. Since 1994, Leeway has recognized painters, fiction writers, and photographers. This year's grants are to fiber artists. Future grants will be awarded in creative non-fiction (1998), sculpture (1999), and painting (2000).

By this autumn, Leeway will have awarded over $250,000 to more than 40 individual women artists — and we are only beginning. I know Grandmom Bessie would be pleased.

Felicity R.S. Benoliel

Among my earlier recollections is a fascination with painting and sculpture, which surrounded me in my parents' and grandparents' homes. Later I realized that most of the paintings were by my grandfather, Julian Story, and the sculpture by my grandmother, W.W. Story. This early exposure contributed to a love of art that has endured and grown over the years.

My desire to help young people led me to the field of teaching for 18 years, and eventually to the University of the Arts (formerly the Philadelphia College of Performing Arts). My position entailed development activities and arranging showcases for young musicians, which proved to be the catalyst for Creative Artists' Network (CAN). The visual arts and assisting young people had been the most prominent elements in my working life. The two were fused through the formation of CAN.

The realization of CAN's mission, "to promote emerging artists," has been most fulfilling and rewarding.

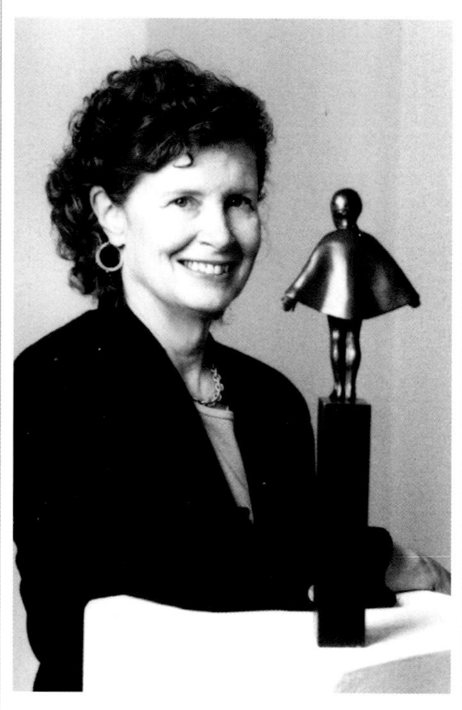

Lifetime Artistic Achievement Award
(first recipient in our Hall of Fame)
Ben Kamihira

In the Order of the Mahlstick
Linda Lee Alter
Felicity R.S. Benoliel

**Fellowship Centennial Exhibition
Awards and Prizes**

Jurors: Luis Cruz Azaceta, Philip
Pearlstein, and Sylvia Yount

*Pennsylvania Academy of the Fine
Arts/Fellowship Purchase Prize*
Barry Goldberg

*The Fellowship of the Pennsylvania
Academy of the Fine Arts Award*
(artistic excellence in any medium
recognizing the concern for human
dignity)
Mike Cockrill

Mary Butler Memorial Award
(any medium)
Baily Bellenger Cypress

Lucy Glick Memorial Award
(excellence in any medium)
Heiko Blankenstein

Percy M. Owens Memorial Award
(distinguished Pennsylvania artist)
Sam Maitin

*Sandra Wolfe Karlin Memorial
Award* (excellence in any medium
will be given each year to a man or
woman who has studied or is studying at the Academy after having had
a career in homemaking, business,
or a profession)
Peggy Gyulai

Catherine Gibbons Granger Award
(painting)
Brett Bigbee

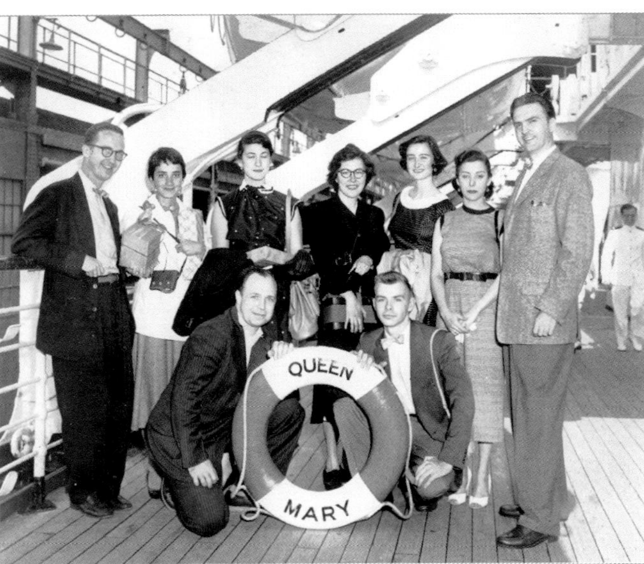

The 1954
Academy
scholarship
winners on
their voyage
to Europe

*Leona Karp Braverman Memorial
Award* (sculpture)
Stephen C. Layne

Berthe M. Goldberg Memorial Award
(any medium)
Judith Silverman Jacobson

*Mabel Wilson Woodrow Memorial
Award* (three undergraduate
students)
Heiko Blankenstein
Rita Klinger
Victor Letonoff

May Audubon Post Memorial Award
(oil painting or sculpture)
Barry Goldberg

Jack Bookbinder Memorial Award
(painting)
Paul King

Adolph Dioda Memorial Award
(sculpture)
Sarah Peters

Award of Merit
(M.F.A. student; any medium)
Ted Zourntos

Riverbank Arts Award
(excellence in any medium)
Ditta Baron Hoeber

Baker's Street Award
(any medium,"Bread of the Month")
Tom King

Fellowship Honorable Mention
Patrick Connors
Nancy M. Jaramillo
Mee Jeong Kim
Joanna Martinez
Eric McDade

**1997 Purchase Awards by the
Fellowship Trust**
The following artists' works were
purchased by the Mary Butler
Memorial Trust Fund of the
Fellowship of the Pennsylvania
Academy of the Fine Arts. These
works are now part of the Fellowship
Collection.
Jurors: Miriam Seidel and Signe
Wilkinson

Jacqueline Cotter*
David S. Dempewolf
Diane S. Grimes
Thomas M. Jackson
Jeff Kellar*
Carolyn Webb
Jim Williams

*represented in exhibition

Thomas W. Golding (1926–1996)
Artist

Mr. Golding was educated at the University of Pennsylvania and the Pennsylvania Academy of the Fine Arts, where he studied with Daniel Garber, Roy C. Nuse, Francis Speight, and others.

His works have been in selected exhibitions in the Philadelphia Museum of Art, the Fellowship of the Pennsylvania Academy of the Fine Arts, the Cheltenham Art Center, the Woodmere Art Museum, and the Abington Art Center, all in the Philadelphia, Pa. area; the Chester County Art Association; Yellow Springs, Pa.; Lancaster, Pa.; Jupiter, Fla.; Tampa, Fla.; and Cape May, N.J.

Thomas Golding had studios in Chalfont, Bucks County, and in Cape May, New Jersey. He received numerous awards for his realistic style in still life and landscapes.

His work is in various collections, such as the Bucks County Bank and Trust Company, and the Cape May Cultural and Historical Commission.

Charles W. Hargens, Jr. (1893–1997)
Artist

Mr. Hargens attended the Pennsylvania Academy of the Fine Arts and Colarossi and Julian Académies, Paris

The artist was the son of Charles W. Hargens, M.D. and Lillian Gamet Hargens, a school teacher. He began his interest in art as early as age six, when he drew charcoal sketches of houses and barns and sold them to neighbors for 25 cents each. He took art classes in high school and worked in the studio of a portrait painter where he heard about the Pennsylvania Academy of the Fine Arts and enrolled in 1914. He won the Cresson Traveling Fellowship for study in Europe, which enabled him to study at the Colarossi and Julian Académies in Paris.

He met Marjorie Garman, a fashion illustrator for ladies' magazines, while studying at the Pennsylvania Academy of the Fine Arts. They were married in 1917; she died in 1978.

Mr. Hargens became known for his painstakingly detailed drawings and paintings of the West. His Western scenes appeared in or on the covers of *The Saturday Evening Post, Colliers', Liberty, McCall's, Boys' Life*, and other magazines, many of which were published in Philadelphia.

He served as a Scoutmaster of Troop 64 in Carversville, Pa., where he and his wife moved in 1949, and was given the Silver Beaver Award by the Bucks County Boy Scout Council in 1953.

He received the Central Bucks Chamber of Commerce Community Service Award for Excellence in Art in 1981.

An honorary Doctor of Fine Arts degree was conferred on him in 1982 from Dakota Wesleyan University of Mitchell, South Dakota.

He had been honored with a special exhibit of his work at the James A. Michener Art Museum in Doylestown, Pa., for his 100th birthday in 1993.

A celebration of his 102nd birthday was held in 1995 by Troop 64, as their appreciation of Mr. Hargens' authorization to sell reproductions of two of his paintings, *Chief Joseph White Bull* and *The Lamplighter*, to raise money to purchase a replacement school bus for scout trips.

Plans are underway by the Friends of the Middle Border Museum to honor him, posthumously, by reconstructing his Carversville studio on the grounds of Dakota Wesleyan University, Mitchell, South Dakota.

He is survived by a son, C.W. Hargens III of Erdenheim, Pa., three grandchildren, and nine great-grandchildren.

Cranston Oliver Walker (1947–1996)
Artist

Mr. Walker was educated in the Philadelphia school system through high school and attended the Pennsylvania Academy of the Fine Arts where he was awarded the William Emlen Cresson Memorial Traveling Scholarship, the Henry Thouron Prize in Composition, and the Charles Toppan Prize for Drawing.

After traveling in Europe on his Cresson Scholarship, Cranston had this to say about his work: "Due to my experience in Europe, I developed a need to approach my art differently. It was then that I started developing concepts using found, unorthodox, and other materials. From these concepts derived a language which is kinetically rooted. I am presently using this language in collage and painting, as well as other mediums."

His works have been exhibited at: Lincoln University, New York City, N.Y.; the Pennsylvania Academy of the Fine Arts and the school's former Peale House Gallery, the Philadelphia Museum of Art, the Walnut Street Theatre, the Museum of the Philadelphia Civic Center, the Woodmere Art Museum, the Philadelphia Art Alliance, Eastern College, all in Philadelphia, Pa.; the DeCordova Museum, Lincoln, Mass.; as well as in the *American Exhibiting Artists* traveling exhibition.

Cranston Oliver Walker was a compassionate, kind, and gentle person.

Ben Wolf (1914–1996)
Artist, Writer, Critic, Teacher

Mr. Wolf received private training with Carl Nordstrom, Arthur B. Carles, and Hans Hofmann.

He was an art critic and columnist, a biographer of artists, an art teacher and lecturer, and a publisher and editor of art magazines.

Ben Wolf studied and taught at the Pennsylvania Academy of the Fine Arts. "He was a general, all-around Renaissance man with a deep committed interest in the arts in general," said Peter Paone, Philadelphia artist and Academy teacher. Frederick S. Osborne, Dean of the Pennsylvania Academy of the Fine Arts, says of Mr. Wolf, "As a person, he was a humanist.... He was a very cultured gentleman, and as such, he symbolized a whole era here at the academy...."

Mr. Wolf worked in oils, pen-and-ink drawings, silk screening, but was best known for his watercolors.

He wrote a column for the *Jewish Exponent* and was publisher of *Philadelphia Art News*. He was also the biographer of two Philadelphia artists, Franklin Watkins and Morton Schamberg.

Mr. Ben Wolf is survived by his wife, Ruth White Wolf, a daughter, three sons, and eight grandchildren.

Sam MAITIN

It is an honor to present this year's Percy M. Owens Memorial Award to one of Philadelphia's own respected and re-nowned artists, Mr. Sam Maitin.

Mr. Maitin was born on October 26, 1928 to Russian immigrant parents, who owned a North Philadelphia grocery store. The second of three sons, he attended public school in Philadelphia and won an art scholarship while at Gratz High School to attend the Philadelphia Museum School of Industrial Arts (now the University of the Arts). At the same time, he enrolled as a part-time student at the University of Pennsylvania, where he received his bachelor's degree in 1951. He married Lilyan Miller in 1964 and has two children, a son and a daughter.

He is an active member and exhibitor with the Philadelphia Print Club and is one of the founding artist members of the *Prints in Progress* program. Mr. Maitin headed the Graphic Communications Laboratory of the Annenberg School of Communications at the University of Pennsylvania, and was Graphic Director and consultant for the Arts Council of the YM/YWHA, all in Philadelphia, Pa.

Mr. Maitin has taught variously at local art institutions, including the Philadelphia College of Art, Moore College of Art, and the Philadelphia Museum of Art.

Early in his career he was awarded the Guggenheim Fellowship Award for travel in England and also the National Etching Award from the Philadelphia Print Club.

On the lecture circuit, he was invited as a guest lecturer to speak about site-specific artworks at Kent Institute of Art and Design in Canterbury, England, and at Camberwell School of Art in London. He later lectured on Public Art in Miami, Florida, and the State of Massachusetts Art Foundation invited Mr. Maitin to judge the 1987 awards grants to Massachusetts artists.

His commissions for mural and sculpture site-specific artworks are very numerous. Some can be viewed at the Free Library of Philadelphia; the Annenberg School of Communications at the University of Pennsylvania; Children's Hospital; Hahnemann Hospital (now known as Allegheny University Hospital); Main Line Reform Temple; Pennsylvania Hospital; and the Temple University Dental School. Many other site-specific works were created by Mr. Maitin for private individuals. Mr.

Maitin's artwork is represented in the permanent collections of the Library of Congress, the National Gallery of Art, the Smithsonian Institution, all in Washington, D.C.; the Museum of Modern Art, New York, N.Y.; the Oakland Museum, California; Currier Gallery of Art, Manchester, N.H.; the Tate Gallery in London, England; the Museum of American Art of the Pennsylvania Academy of the Fine Arts, the University of Pennsylvania, and the Philadelphia Museum of Art, all in Philadelphia, Pa.; and the Picker Museum at Colgate University, Hamilton, N.Y.

He continues to create serigraphs and posters commissioned to celebrate or honor people for special occasions. Some serigraphs given as SANE Awards are owned by Jane Fonda, Tom Hayden, Bishop Desmond Tutu, Dr. Helen Caldicott, Carl Sagan, Rev. Jesse Jackson, and other celebrities.

Many of Mr. Maitin's works have been exhibited around the world — in France, England, Germany, Poland, Israel, Japan, China, Mexico, and in the United States from coast to coast.

His biographical sketch is listed in the 1997 Edition of *Who's Who in America.*

Throughout his career, Mr. Maitin has produced an exorbitant amount of work. The result is a world-wide recognition of his name in the art world.

Mr. Sam Maitin is well-deserving of the Percy M. Owens Memorial Award that the Fellowship of the Pennsylvania Academy of the Fine Arts is presenting to him this year.

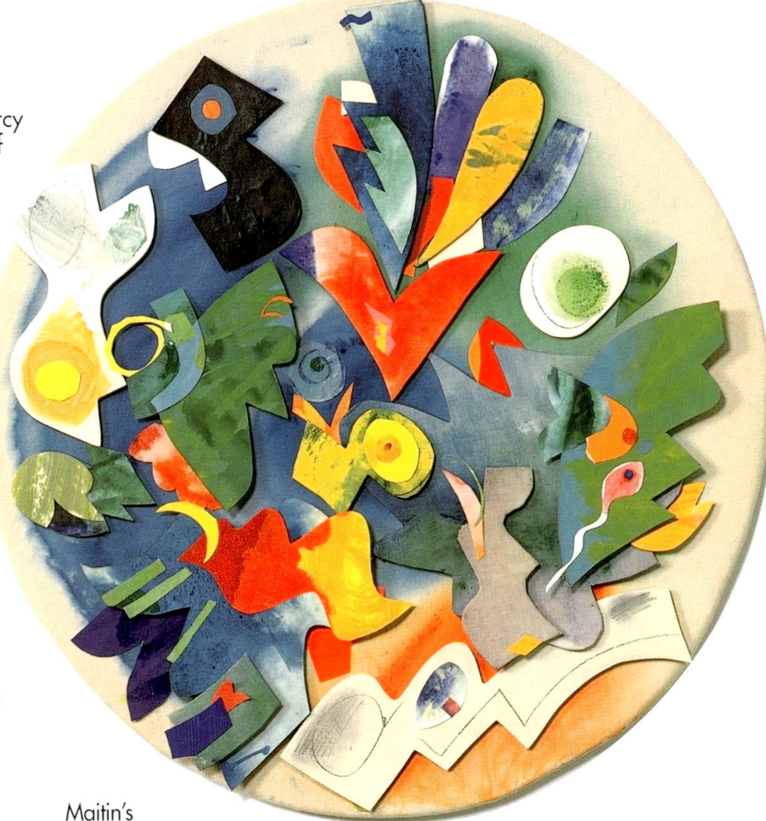

Dulcifier I, 1997 Dimensional collage, watercolor, acrylic, paper, and wood on canvas, 36" dia. Courtesy of the artist

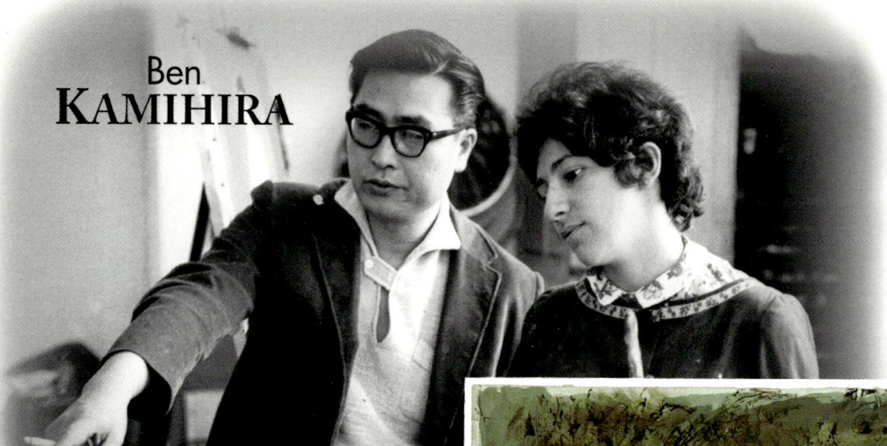

Ben KAMIHIRA

Ben Kamihira with student, c.1960

Two Women, 1995-96
Watercolor with Chinese White, 19 x 20"
Collection of Harriet Kravitz

Ben Kamihira was born on a farm in Yakima, Washington, March 16, 1925. His mother died when he was fourteen years old. Two years later, in 1941, after Pearl Harbor was bombed, Ben and his family were sent to a relocation center, and later to eastern Oregon to work as farm laborers.

After high school, Ben was inducted into the army, joining the famed Japanese American 442nd Unit. When the war ended, he was chosen for selective training in Florence, Italy, and thus was able, for the first time in his life, to go to a museum and receive drawing instruction.

When he was discharged from the army, Ben enrolled at the Art Institute of Pittsburgh. After a year there, he applied to and was accepted at the Pennsylvania Academy of the Fine Arts. During the next four years, Ben felt he had found a home. He had great respect for Joseph Fraser, the Director, and he felt privileged to have his work criticized by the likes of Daniel Garber, Franklin Watkins, Roswell Weidner, Francis Speight, Walter Stuempfig, and Hobson Pittman. He formed close relationships with his teachers (Roswell Weidner is a good friend to this day) and fellow students, especially Jimmy C. Lueders and Paul Kramer, a well-known Minneapolis/St. Paul artist, teacher, and collector. While Ben was still a student, the Fellowship of the Pennsylvania Academy purchased one of his paintings, *The Nuns*, which they generously donated to the permanent collection of the Academy's Museum. Thereafter, Ben joined the faculty of the Academy where, over the next 25 years, he attracted many talented young artists to his classes.

Ben never really felt he was an artist in the true sense of the word until he went to Spain on a Guggenheim Grant in 1956. He fell in love with it from the very first day and as the years have gone by his feelings have only increased. He has spent much of his adult life in Spain, alternating

between living there and in Philadelphia. Many of his best canvases were painted in Spain and its influence is still apparent in his work today.

By 1979, it was evident that the Academy was going in a new direction. As the result of a disagreement with the Director of the School, Ben's contract was not renewed; with both relief and regret, he found his teaching days at the Academy were over. Because he was no longer bound by a teaching schedule, over the next decade he was able to remain in Spain, painting for long periods of time.

Ben has been married twice and has nine children. He has traveled extensively in Europe, went to Japan (for his first and only visit) on a National Endowment for the Arts Grant, and still continues to go to his studio every day. Several years ago, while recovering from an operation, he switched from oil painting to watercolors. He was surprised and not displeased with his efforts, although for him, watercolors will never replace oils.

Elizabeth S. Kamihira

Lorraine
ALEXANDER

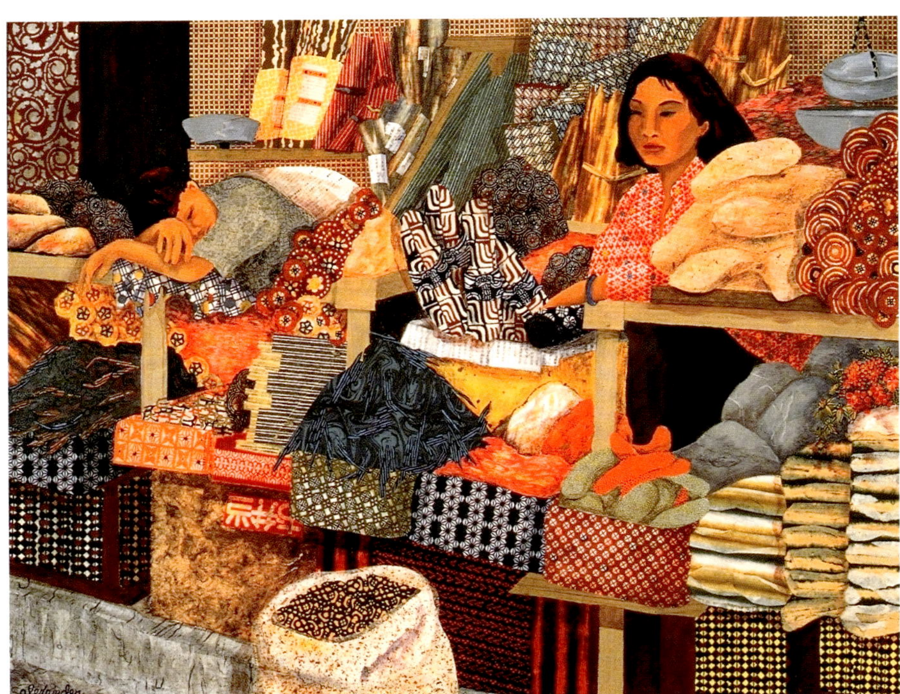

I have collected handmade papers in my travels through-out the world from Africa to New York. I am fascinated with the interplay of subject, form, color, and patterns coming together like pieces of an intriguing puzzle. With photography, I record inspir-ing moments, and later incorporate them into my creative compositions.

Xian: Market
Mixed collage and oil paint,
30 x 40"
Private collection

Eleanor
ALLEN

Jessica was my husband's sister; a beautiful young woman even in death. While the cancer disfigured her body, it didn't damage her spirit. She fought it until the last day of February, 1995.

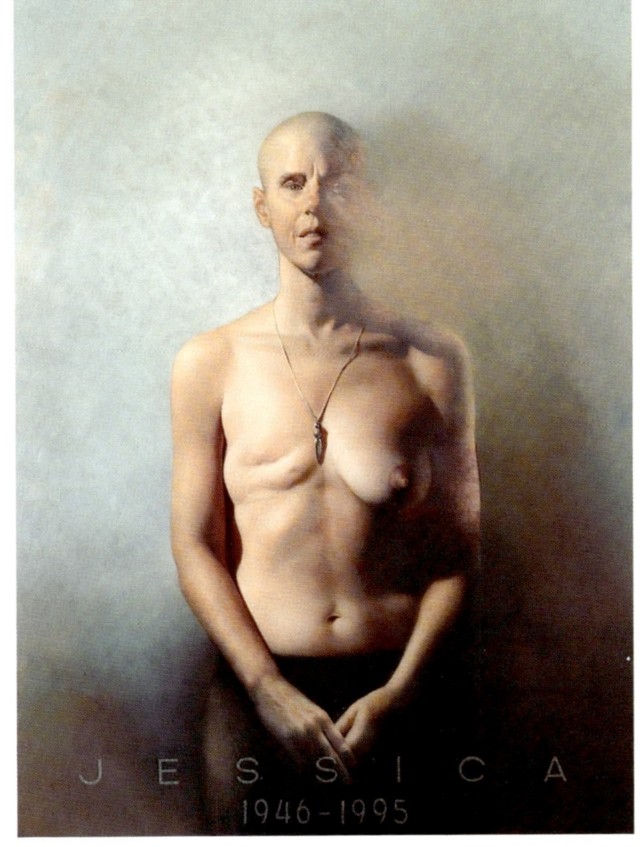

Jessica
Oil on linen, 42 x 32"

Jock
ANDERSON

The Homecoming
Oil on linen, 40 x 50"

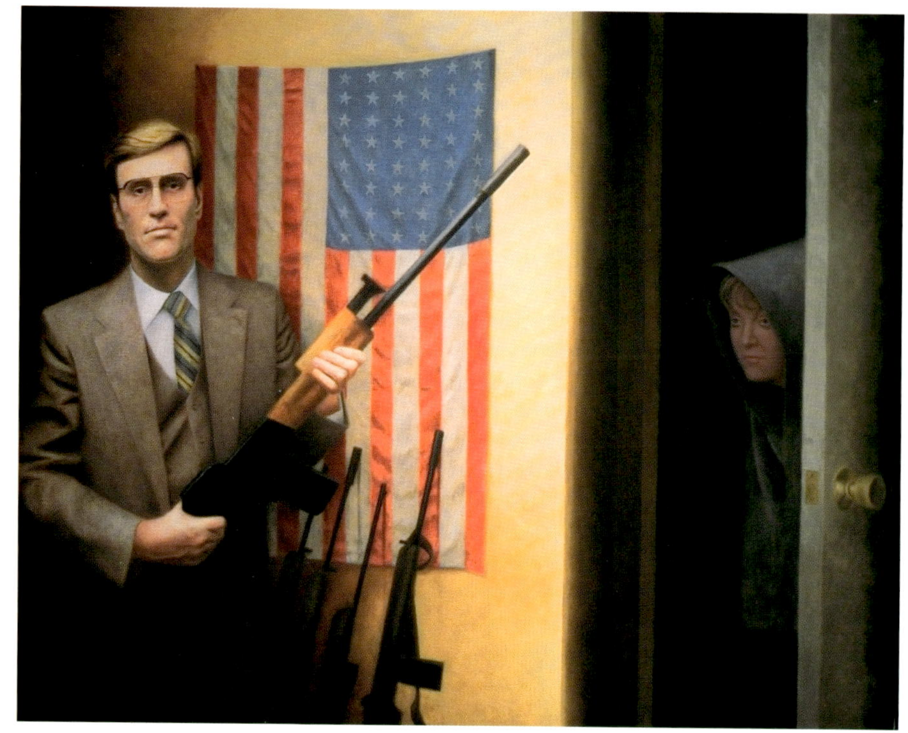

Dennis
AUFIERY

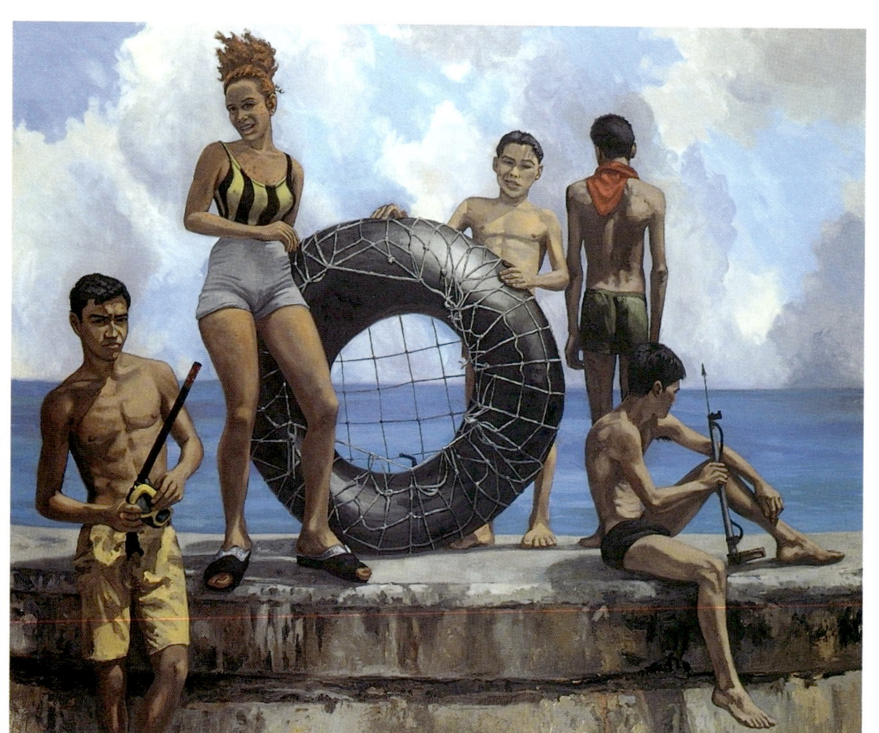

*I like art that is like
peeling an onion.*

There are many layers.

Balseros, Havana
Oil on canvas, 65 x 80"

Pinwheel
Charcoal and graphite,
70 x 45"

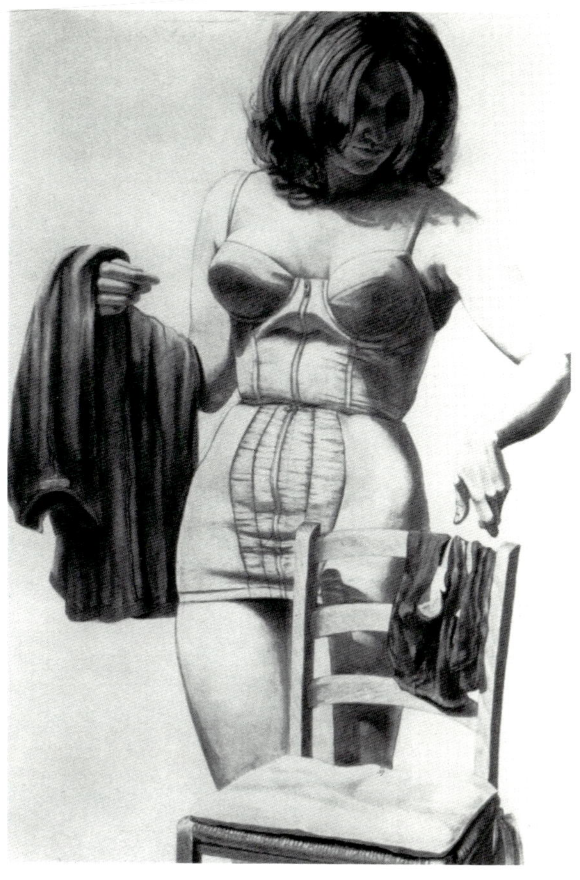

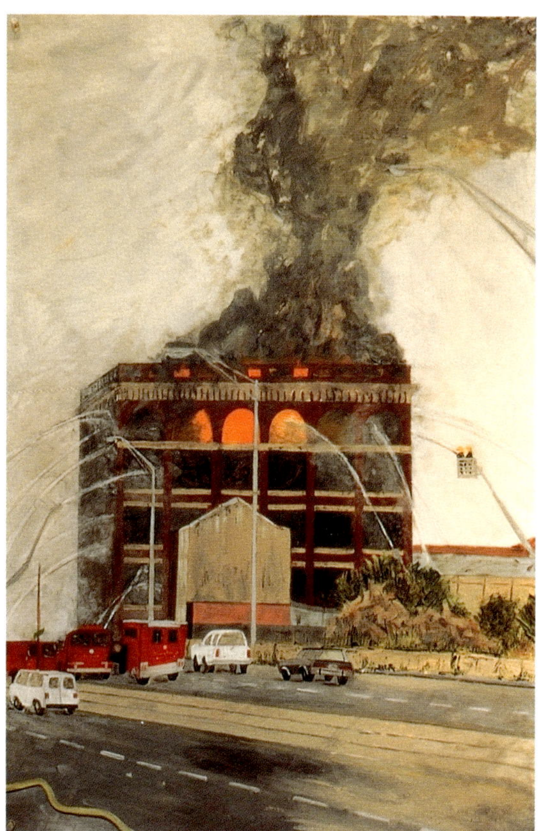

*American Street in Philadelphia,
once one of the great manufactur-
ing districts of the world, has
been in the process of burning
and collapsing over the past two
decades. My monoprints, done
rapidly to capture the immediacy
of disintegration, represent a kind
of visual diary of demolition and
decay; images of a vanishing city.*

Warehouse Burning, American Street
Oil on mylar, 39 x 26"

Joseph
BARBIERI

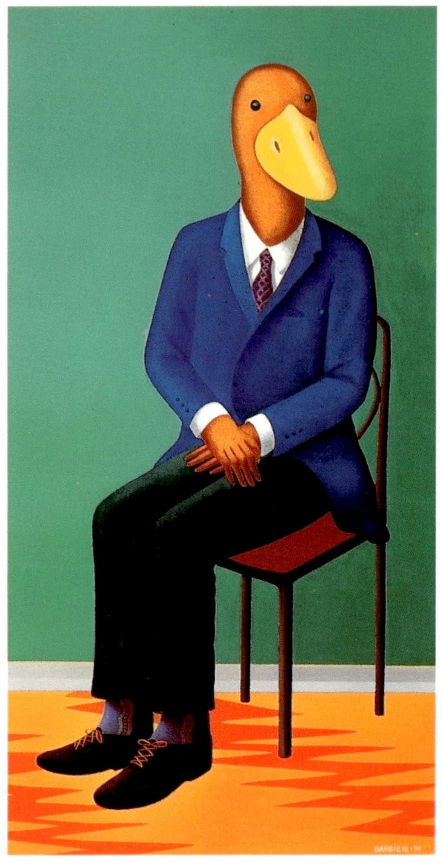

Commission
Oil on canvas, 19 x 10"

Robert
BECK

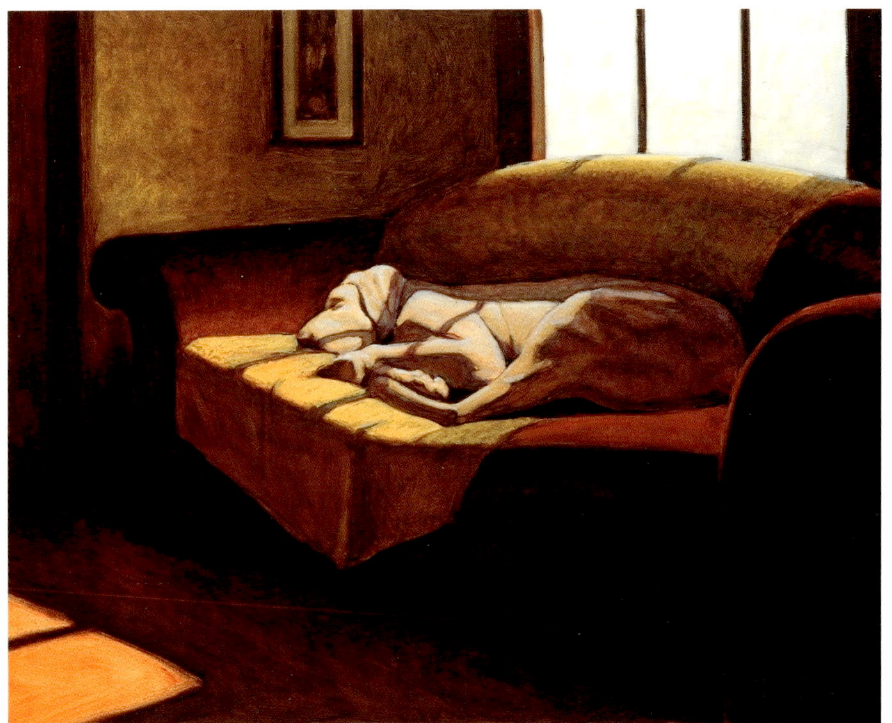

I paint things that are part of my life: companion of a decade, touchstone for things meaningful and sorely missed.

Light Duty
Oil on panel, 24 x 30"

Brother & Sister
Oil, 72 x 48"
Collection of Ms. Richelle Kaufman

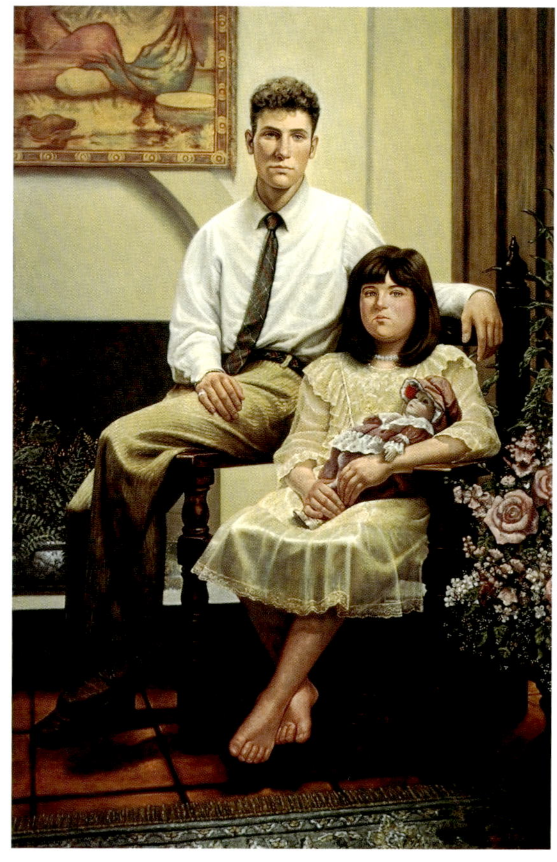

Frank
BENDER

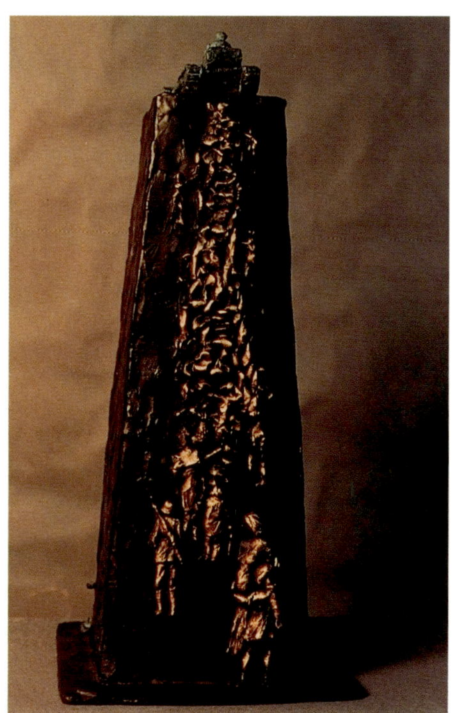

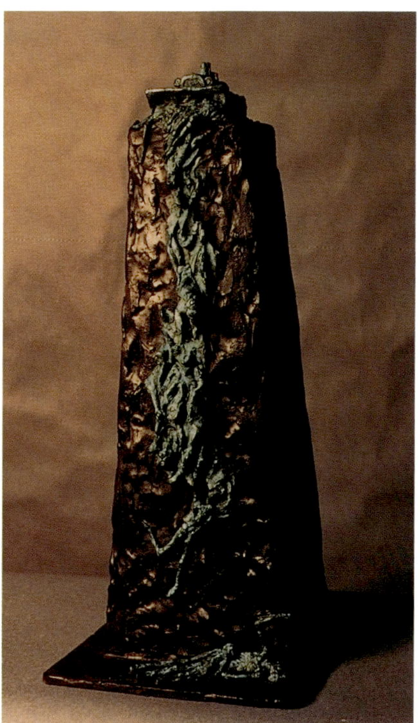

I chose the medium of sculpture for my visual presentation of a Holocaust Memorial, believing that it would inspire curiosity and compassion for those who can no longer speak. May it also stand as a reminder to those of us who can speak that we must always question actions sanctioned by governments, with the support of their citizenry, against any people, lest history repeat itself and spawn another holocaust.

Lest We Forget
Bronze, 22 ½ x 10 x 12"

Stanley
BIELEN

Frustration of Faith
Oil on linen, 24 x 30"
Collection of Jane Barry and
Dr. Patrick O'Kane

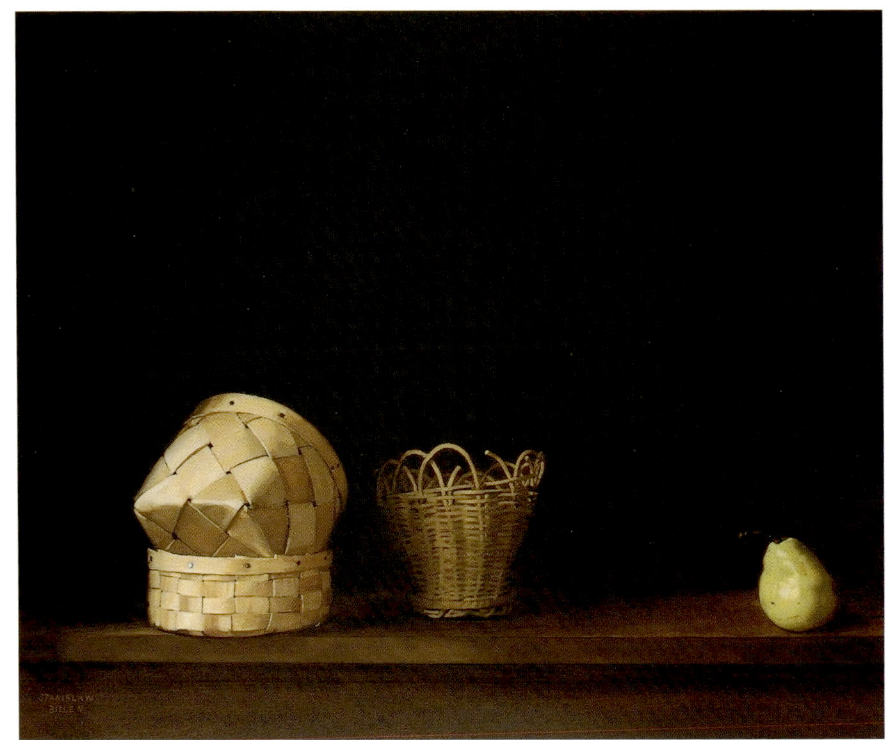

Rachel
BLISS

Miss Lou
Oil and acrylic on canvas,
18 x 14"

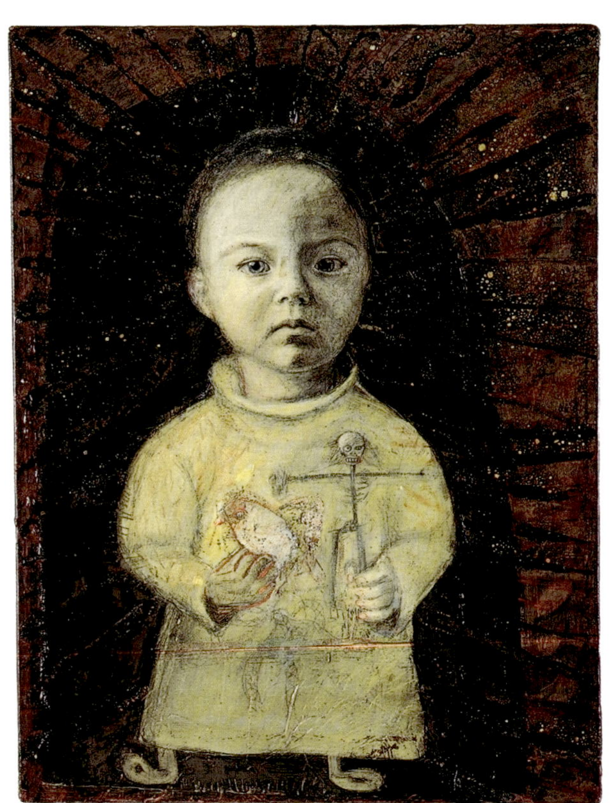

*"And that moment when the
bird sings very close
To the music of what happens."*

— Seamus Heaney

Crime Scene II
Oil on canvas, 54 x 64"

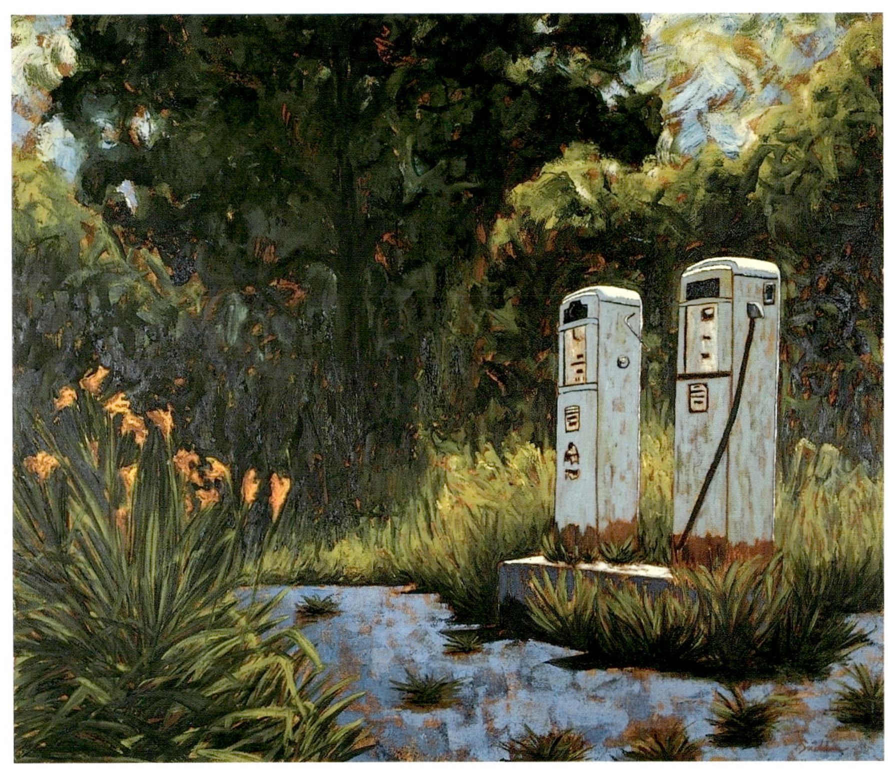

Moe A.
BROOKER

To be still & still moving
Mixed media on BFK paper,
42 x 60"

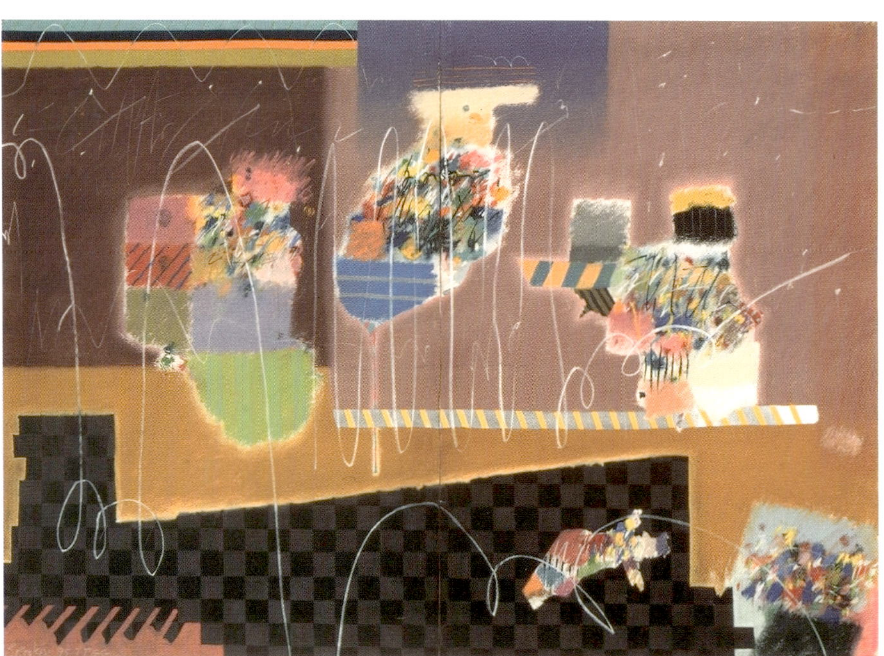

*I begin by mapping out the painting.
After that, I don't know what
happens — I think it has something
to do with being from New Jersey.*

French Doors
Latex and cement on canvas,
81 x 55"

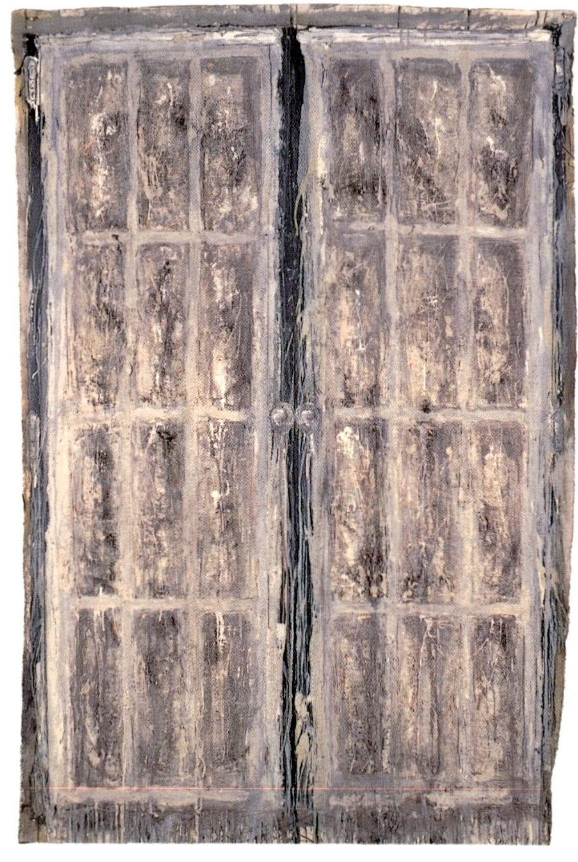

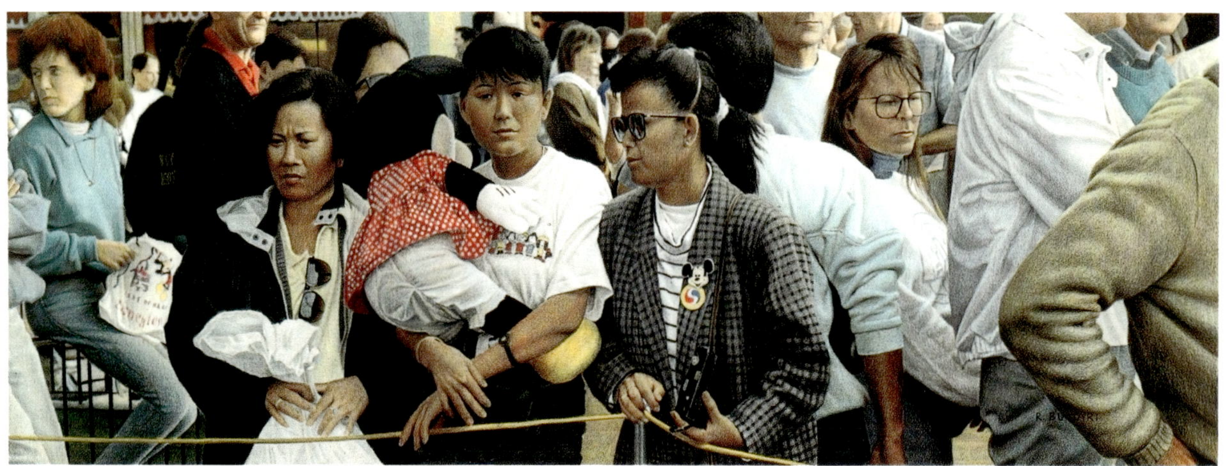

Crowd Scene with Minnie Mouse
Colored pencil on illustration board, 21 x 34"

Philip J. CARROLL

This series of paintings is an exploration of the abstract and sculptural qualities of man-made objects found in nature. The objects that man creates are far more revealing of his soul than the man himself.

Open
Oil on linen, 42 x 26"

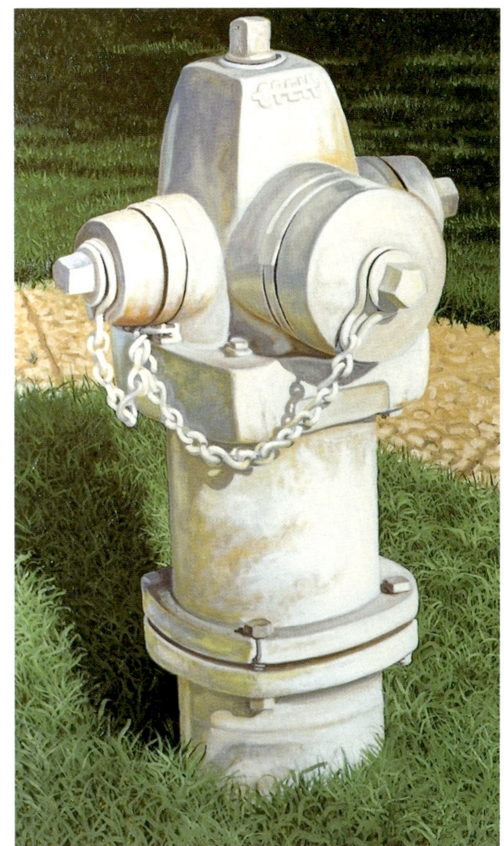

Giovanni CASADEI

The encounter of the two natures — the so-called "nature" outside of myself, and the nature of the painter — gives birth to my paintings. I'm always amazed at how a few brush strokes on a small flat surface can reduce and confine the complexity and the completeness of "nature." Still, we recognize a painting born of this process as "reality" and more: it is the reality that contains the painter's inner nature.

Self-Portrait
Oil on canvas, 30 x 26"

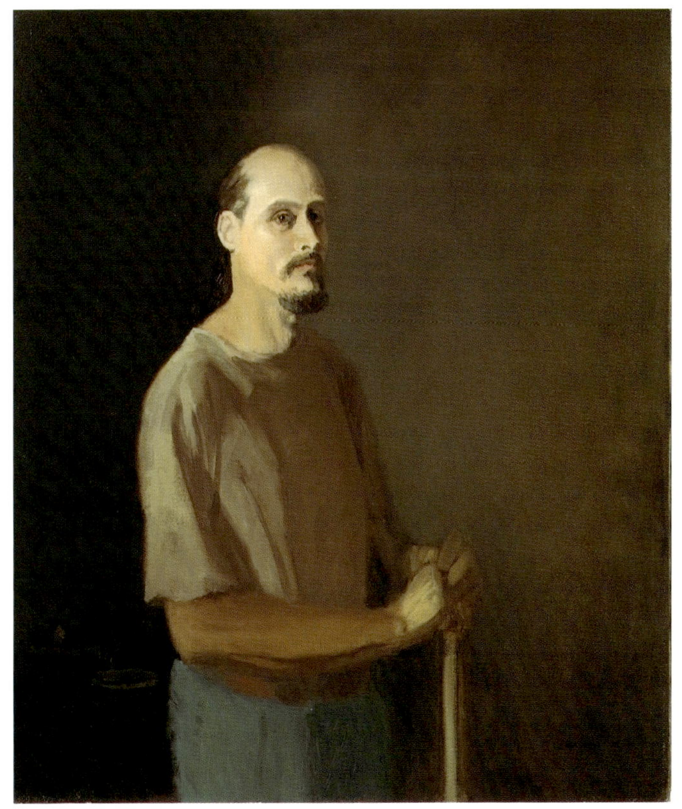

Nancy
CITRINO

A Suitable Man
Monotype, 20 x 16"

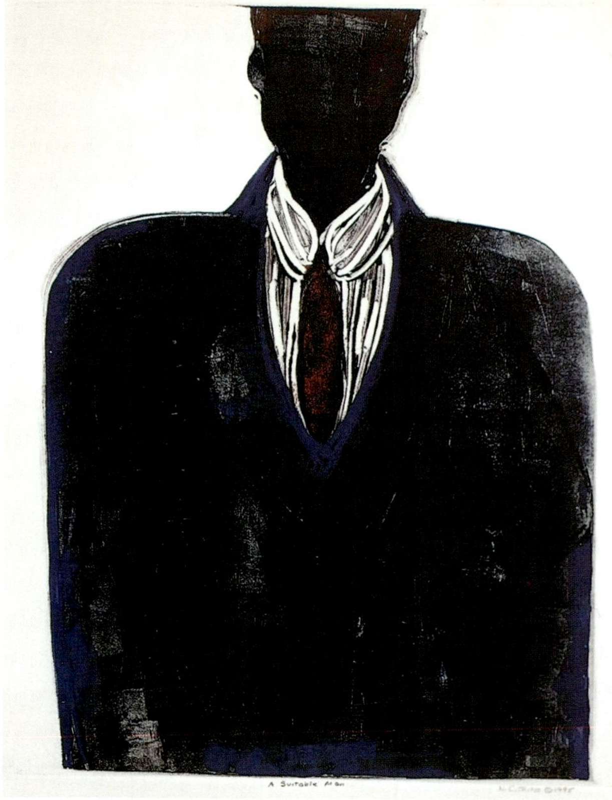

Beth Lea
CLARDY

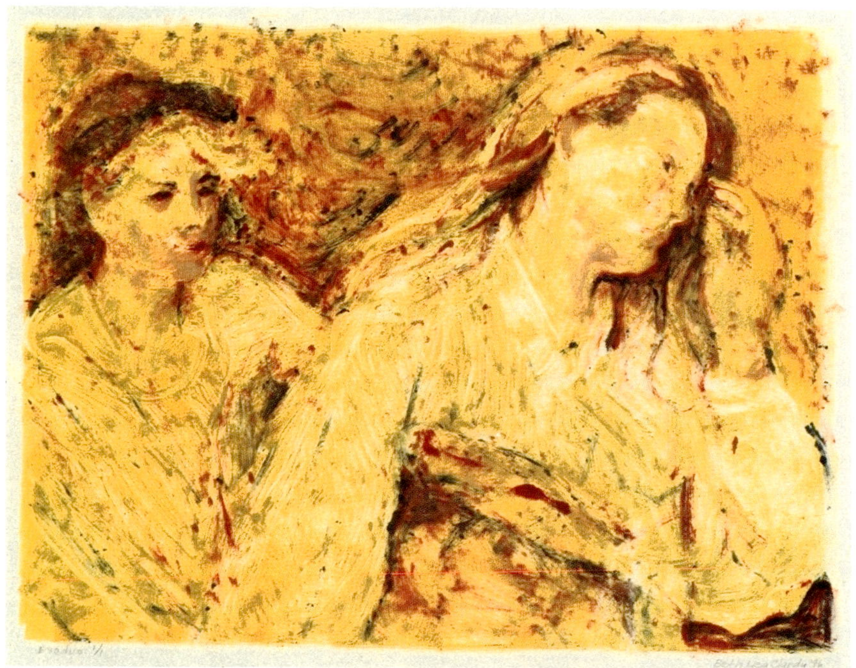

I have come to monoprint-
ing late in life and find
my best expression in it.
My subject matter is
people — singly or reacting
in some way as a pair.

Exodus
Monoprint, 22 x 20"

Mike
COCKRILL

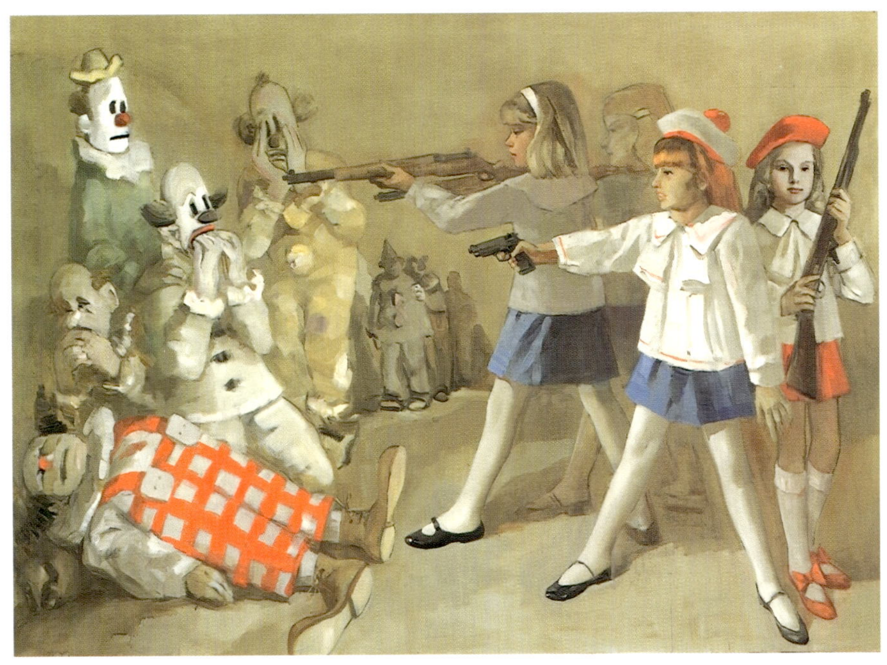

*"Independence Day"
was inspired by
my childhood memories
of clown paintings,
girls' fashion, and
wartime execution
photographs, as well
as by Goya and Manet.
The painting is in-
tended to examine our
moral response to
genocide by using
ethical ambiguity: who
is really the victim and
who is the victimizer?*

Independence Day
Oil on canvas, 64 x 90"
★ The Fellowship of the
Pennsylvania Academy of
the Fine Arts Award

Patrick
CONNORS

Schuylkill River Bridge
Oil on linen, 48 x 60"

★ Honorable Mention

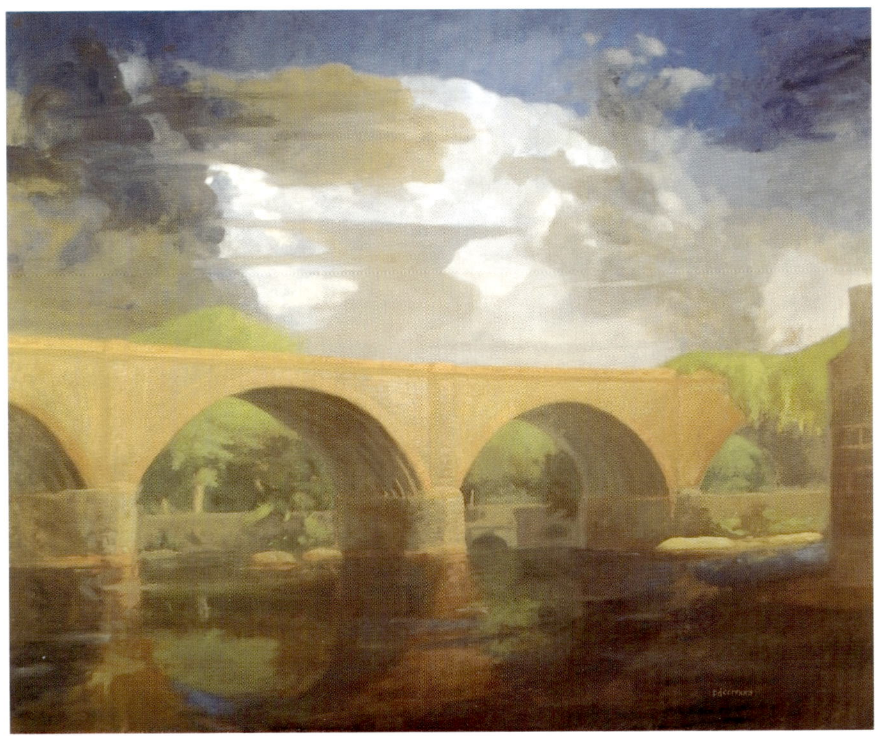

Evergreen
Oil and mixed media on canvas, 40 x 40"

★ Purchase Award by the Fellowship Trust

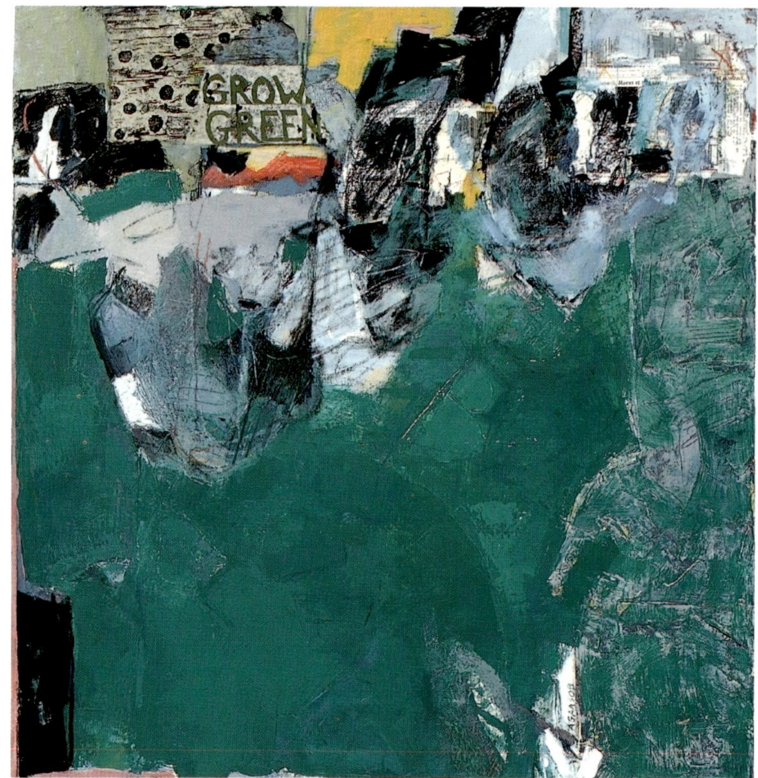

Kevin
CUMMINS

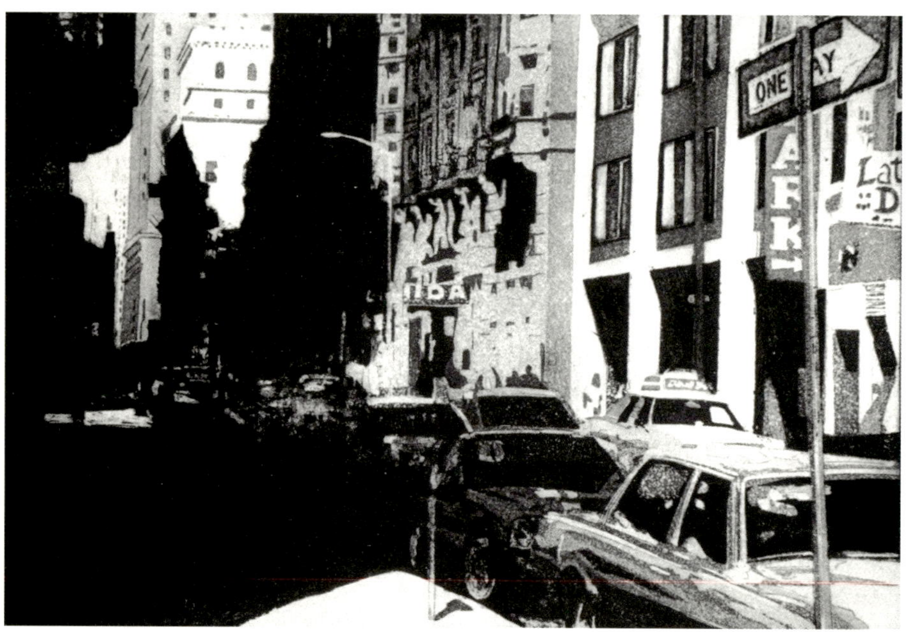

South 15th Street
Etching and aquatint, 6 x 9"

CYPRESS

Innocence Lost (A Memorial)
Mixed media (toy planes, plastic flowers),
120 x 84 x 48"
★ Mary Butler Memorial Award

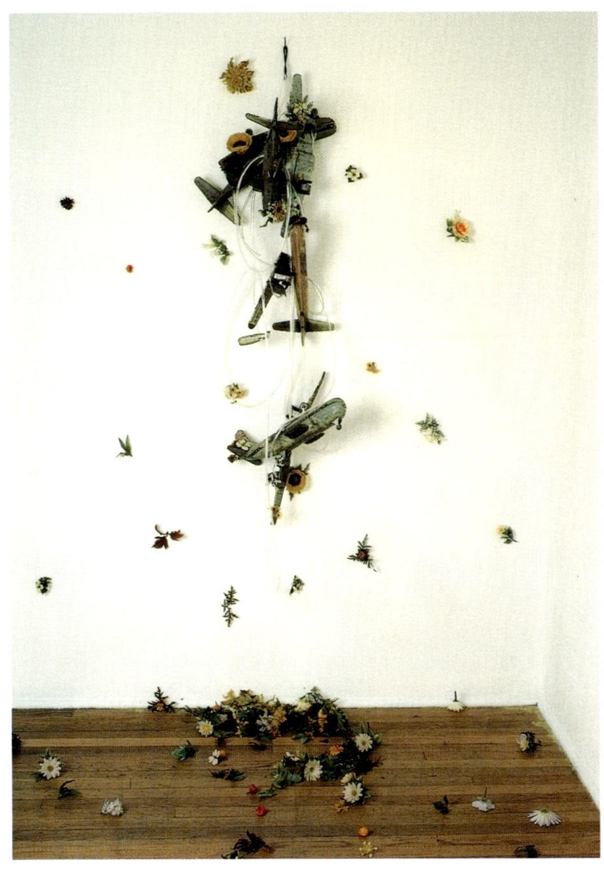

Fred
DANZIGER

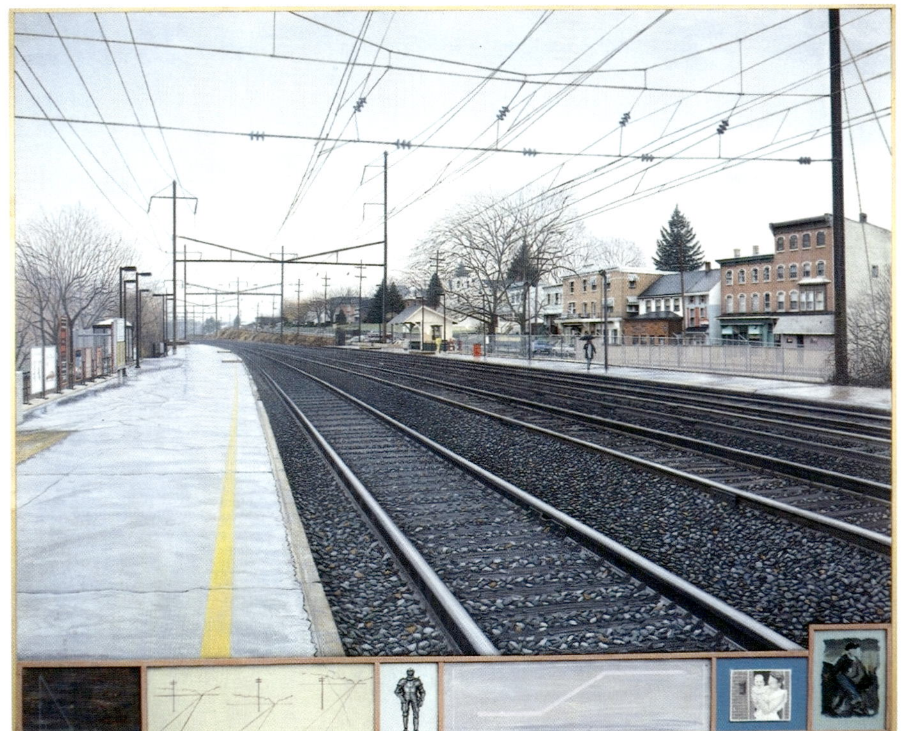

Almost April
Acrylic on canvas,
62 x 74"

Deborah
DEICHLER

A Man Looking Over His Shoulder
Oil on gessoed ragboard on panel,
13 $^5/_8$ x 9 $^7/_8$"

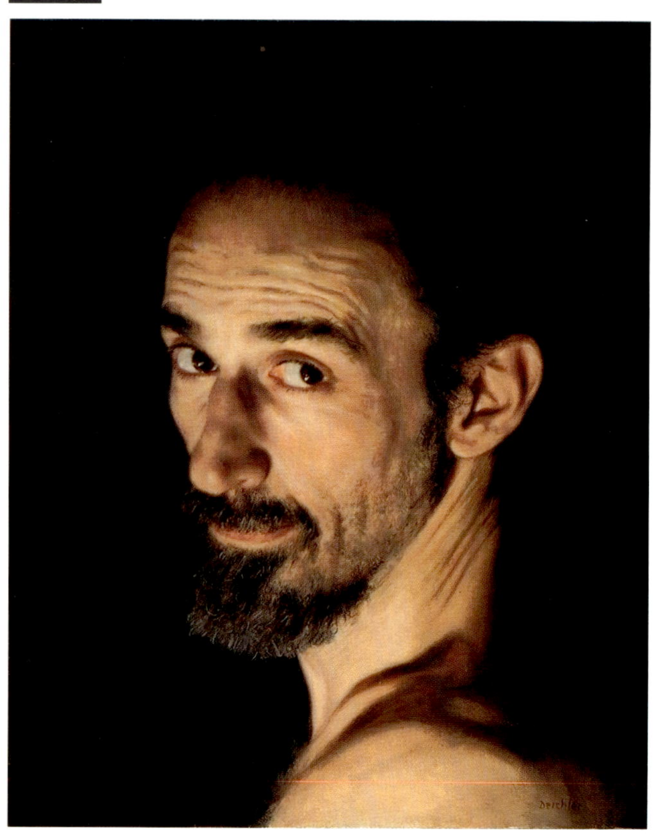

Michael
DELUCA

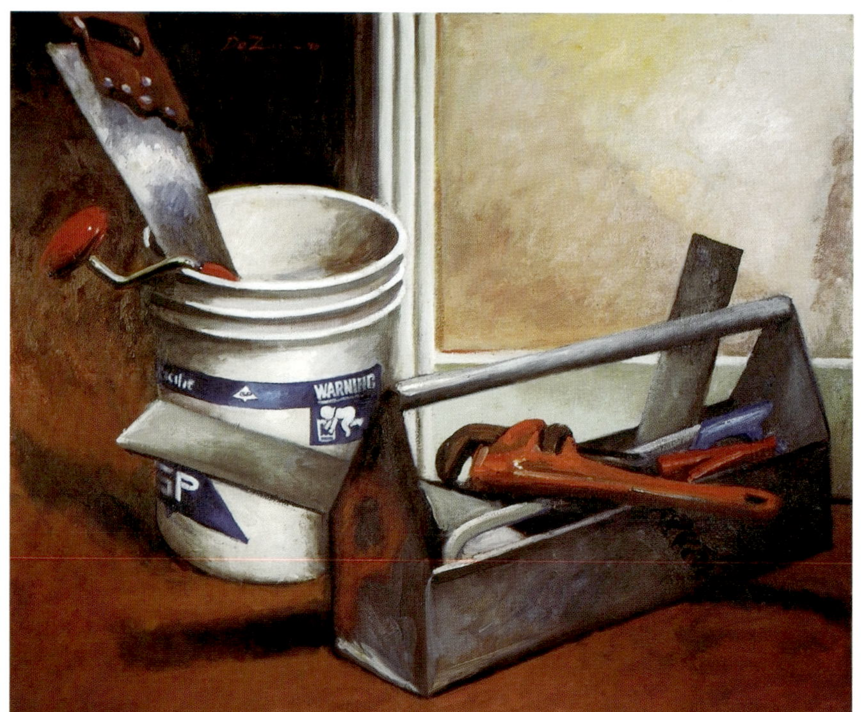

Hand Tool
Oil on canvas, 34 x 40"

Manayunk
Charcoal and graphite on
mounted paper,
7 1/4 x 8 1/4"

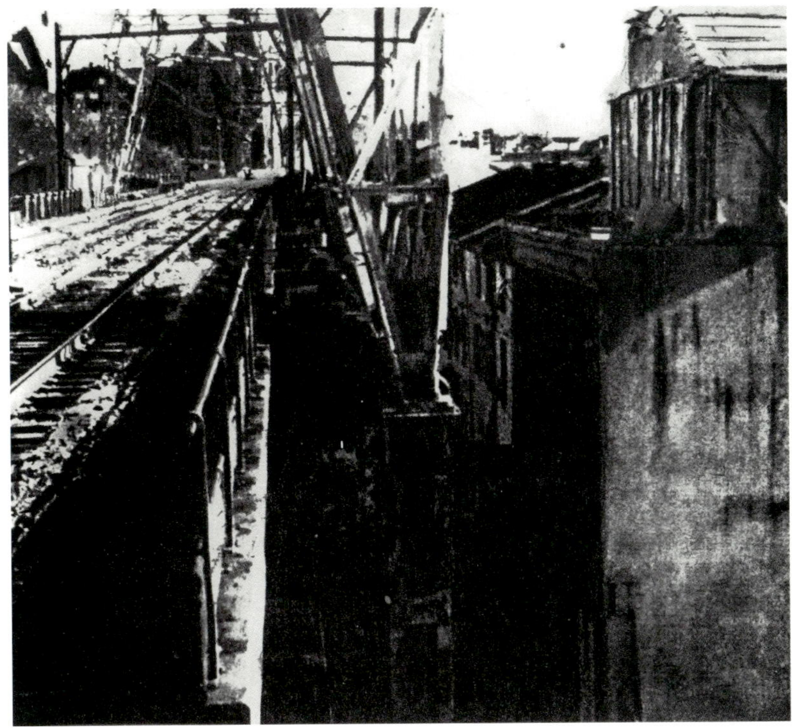

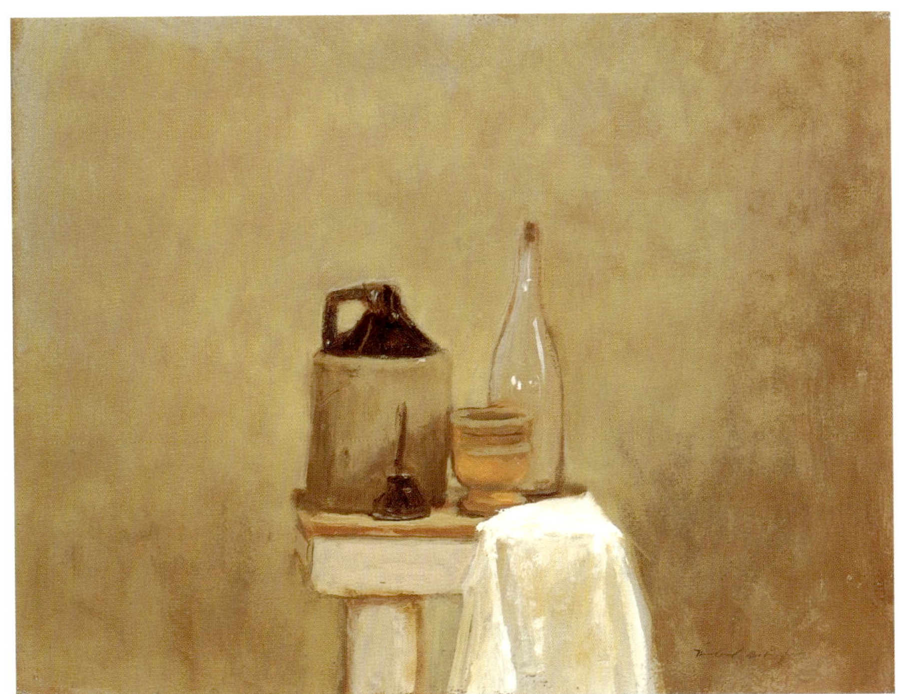

Still Life with Oil Can
Oil on masonite,
7 x 9"

Ann Clardy EKSTROM

*My paintings are composi-
tions of tiny, elderly objects
involved in a dialogue
about memory, attachments,
and the passage of time.*

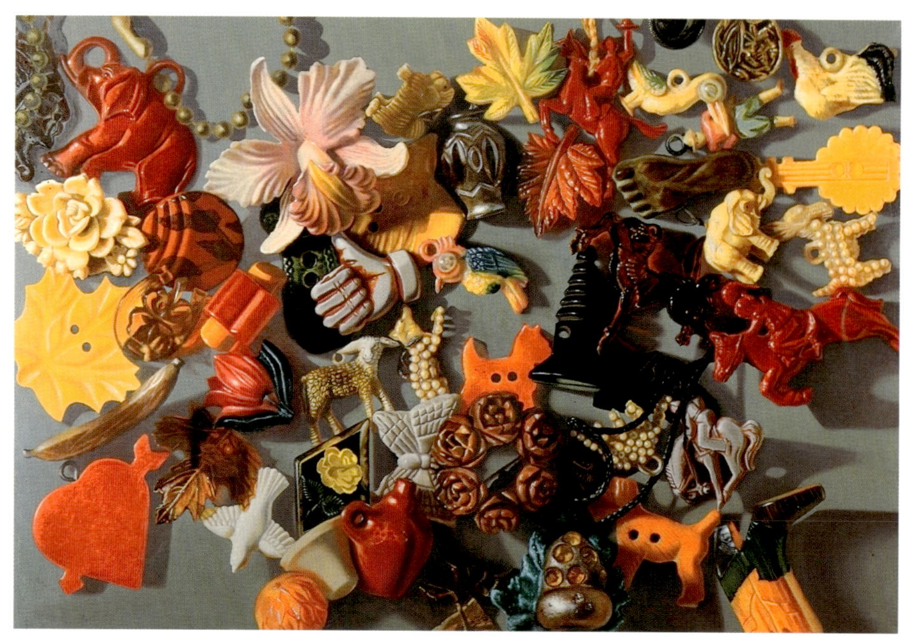

Flora/Fauna Crackerjack
Oil on linen, 48 x 72"

Stephen ESTOCK

The Weight of Things Unsaid
Oil on linen, 48 ¼ x 36"

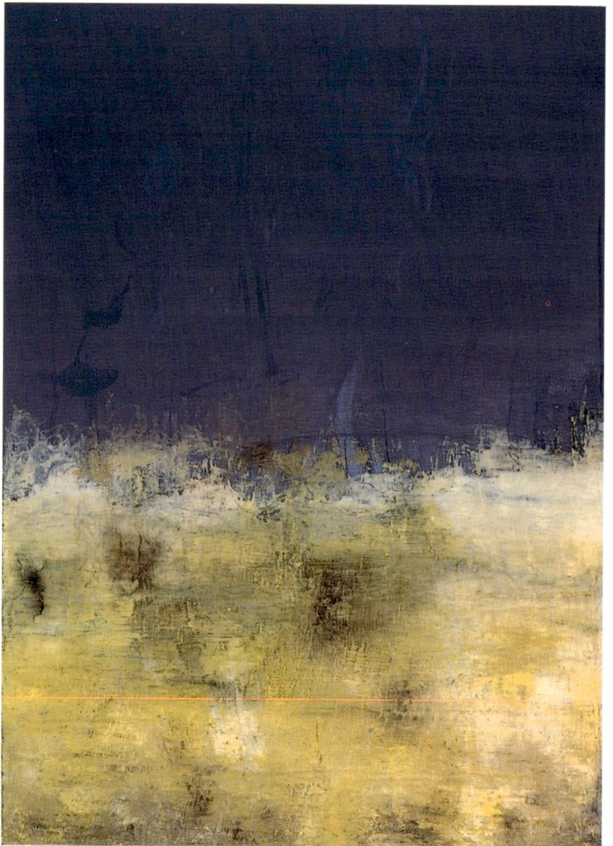

"Out of thy head I sprung. Amazement seized

All th' host of Heaven: back they recoiled afraid

At first, and called me Sin...."

— John Milton
Paradise Lost

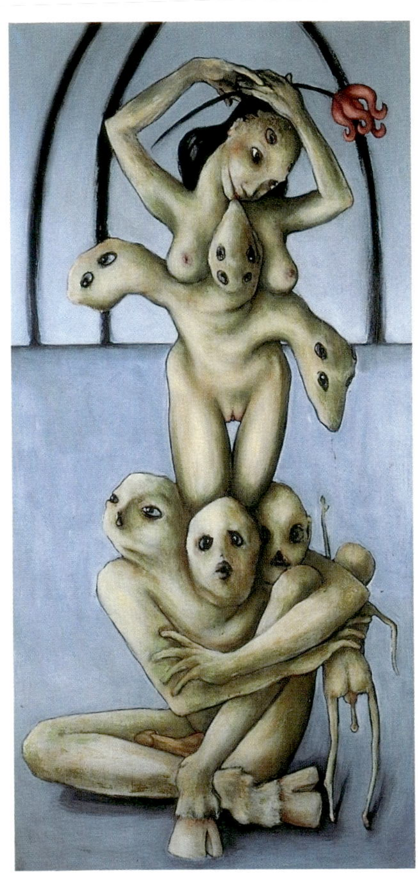

Rape of Satan's Daughter
Oil on canvas, 96 x 48"

Steven
FLOM

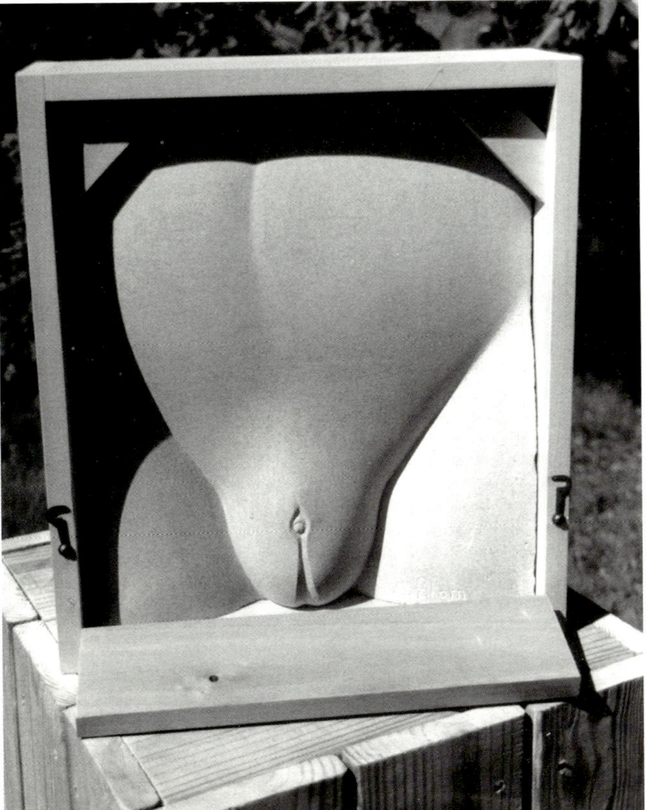

Belly in a Box
Limestone and poplar,
19 x 16 x 6"

FOULKS

Rites of Passage: Limbo
Oil on linen, 72 x 144"

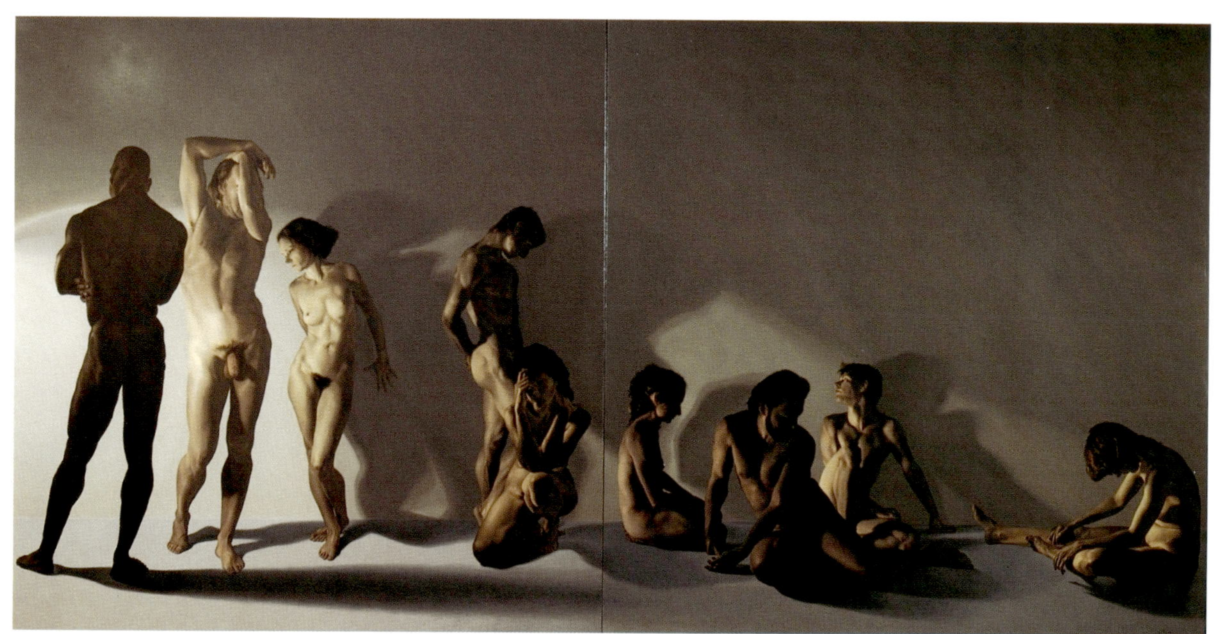

Larry
FRANCIS

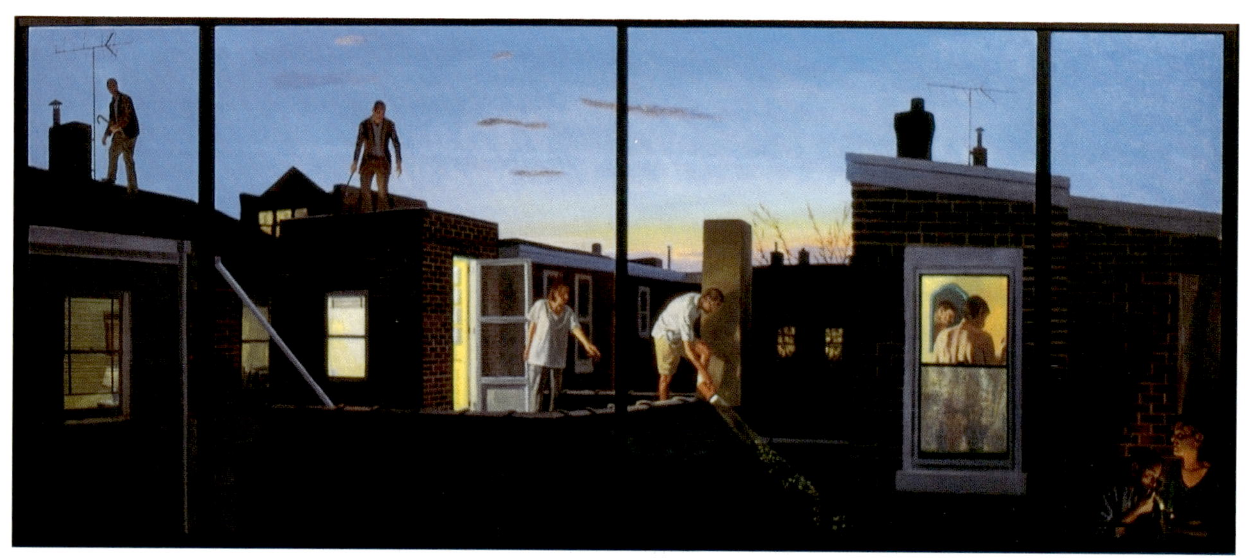

Rooftops
Oil on canvas, 36 ½ x 86"

Joy
Friedman

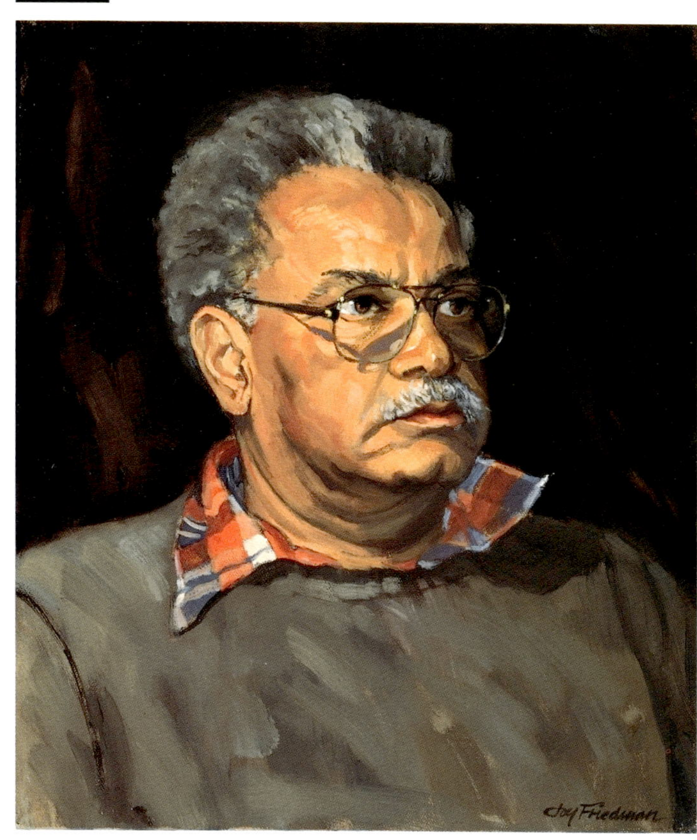

In portraiture, I see each face as an ever-changing map, depicting not only the physical nature of the subject, but reflecting the "geography" of the unique character of the human spirit that lies within.

The Critical Eye—Louis B. Sloan
Oil on canvas, 15 x 13"

Margaretta
Gilboy

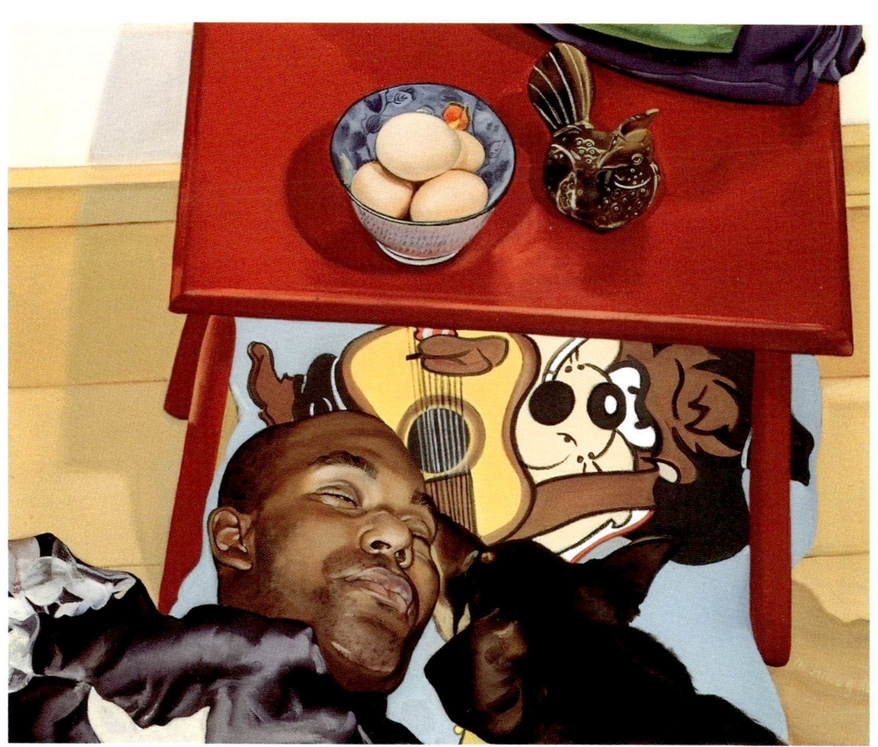

Meaning now lives in the domain of the personal. In my work, meaning is inferred from the dialogue of the components. Continuity and personality are fractured and narrative is discontinuous. Formal value (as in Cubism) and emotional value (as in Expressionism) are reinstated as human value.

Wake Up Call
Oil on linen, 26 x 32"

GOLDBERG

Toothsome
Oil and wax on linen,
55 x 33"
★ Pennsylvania Academy of the
Fine Arts/Fellowship Purchase
Prize and May Audubon Post
Memorial Award

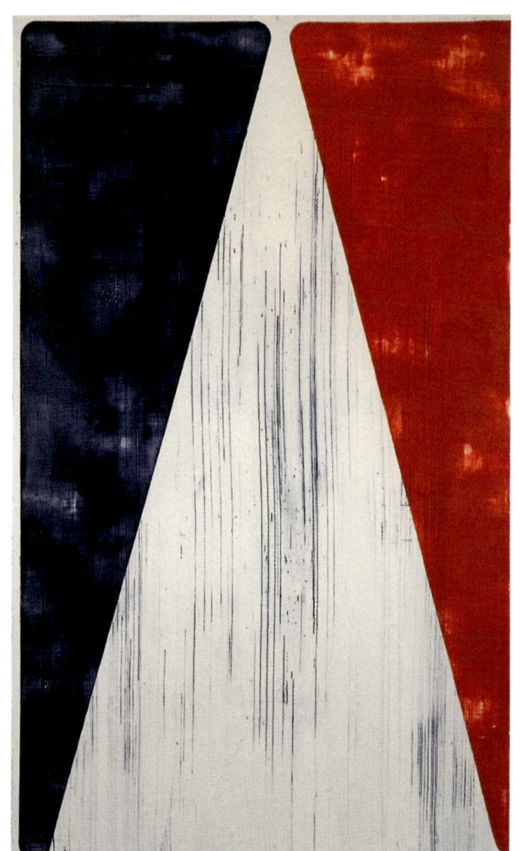

Barbara
GOODSTEIN

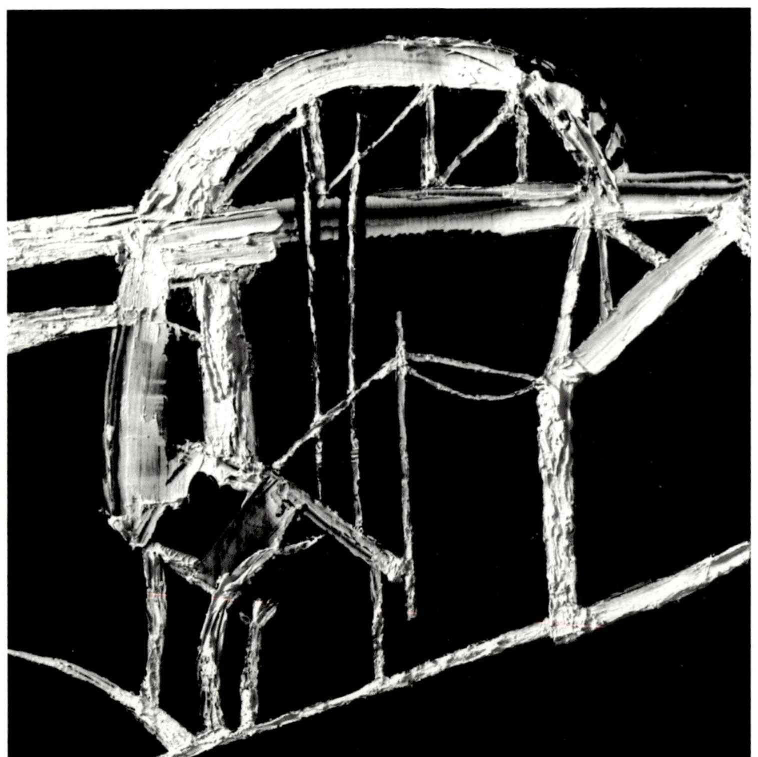

*I wanted relief sculpture
to be thin; to be able to
see through parts of it.
I want to work from
landscape and from
cityscape.*

Railroad Bridge
Modeling paste on painted
board, 22 x 22"

Paul GORKA

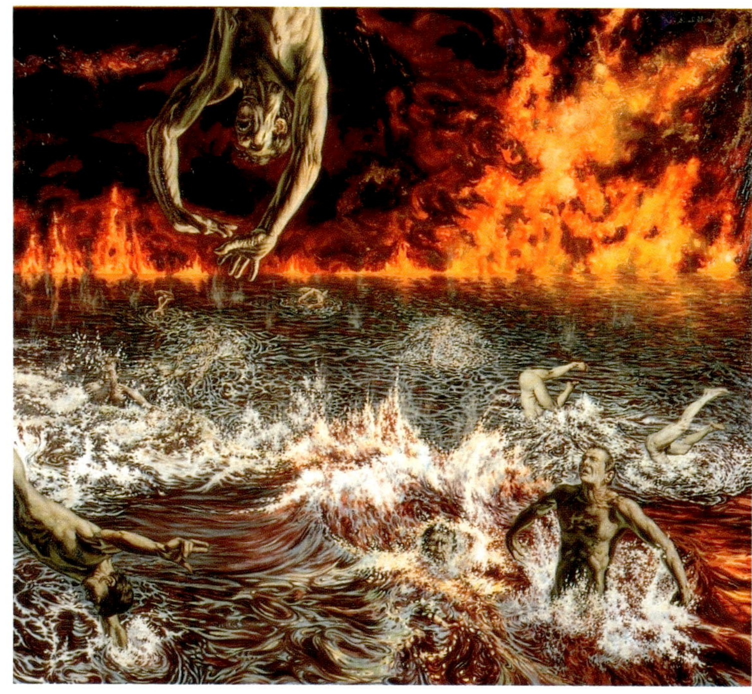

Swimming in Hell
Oil on canvas, 60 x 70"

Peggy GYULAI

The paintings are a meeting place of the worlds of music and land. The painting process is like composing, performing, and conducting a piece, simultaneously. The result is an expression of the shared sensual and emotional qualities I perceive in both the natural world and the world of composed sound — there is no shortage of subject material in sight.

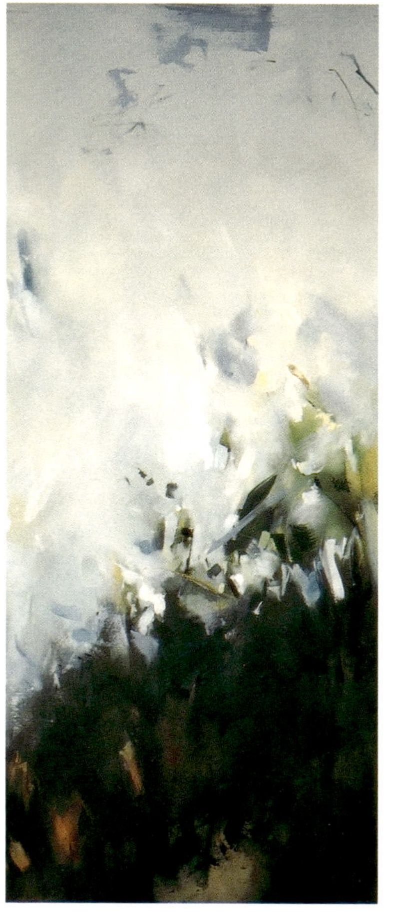

Bartok: Concerto for Orchestra
Oil on canvas, 120 x 48"
★ Sandra Wolfe Karlin Memorial Award

Siegfried
HALUS

I've always been more interested in issues of human consciousness, love, gender, and myth as ways of examining and understanding my place in the world-cosmos. I find myth and its contemporary re-interpretations to be a living stream with a far more significant substance in which to swim than the fixed art theories offered up by artists working with theory-driven motivations.

Untitled
Photography — liquid light emulsion and Polaroid transfer, 17 x 14"

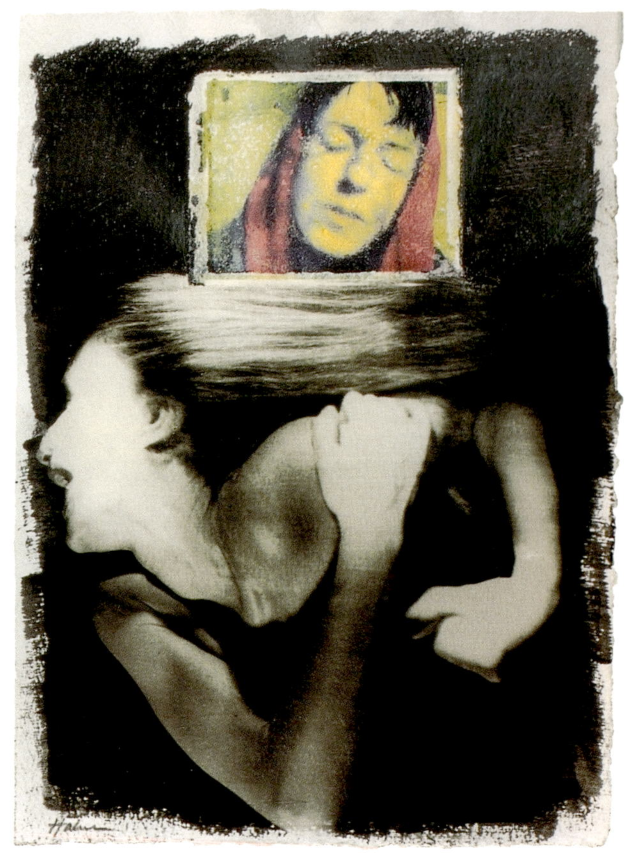

Ditta Baron
HOEBER

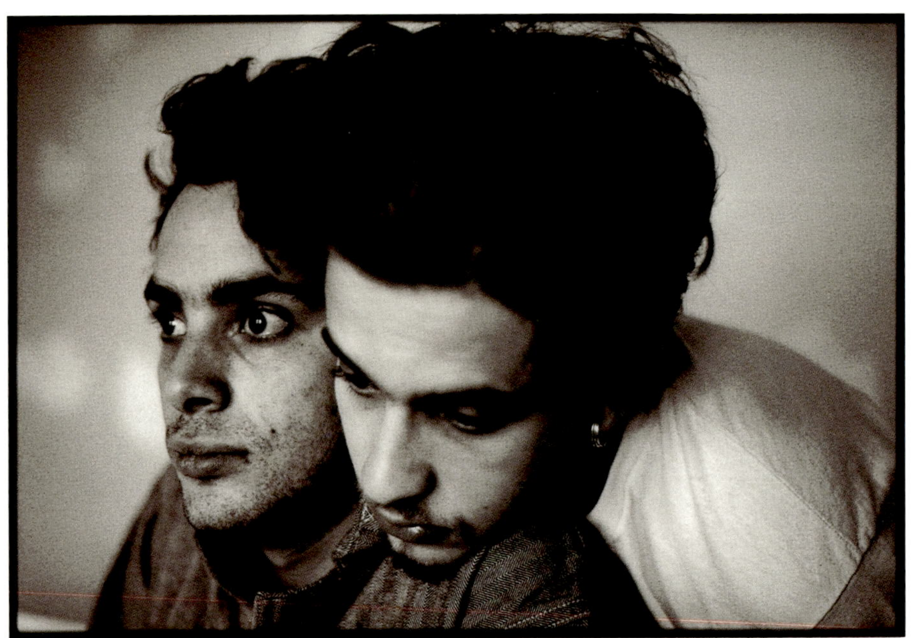

Rose Red, Rose White #22
B & W photograph, 3 1/2 x 5"
★ Riverbank Arts Award

Christopher
HORNBECK

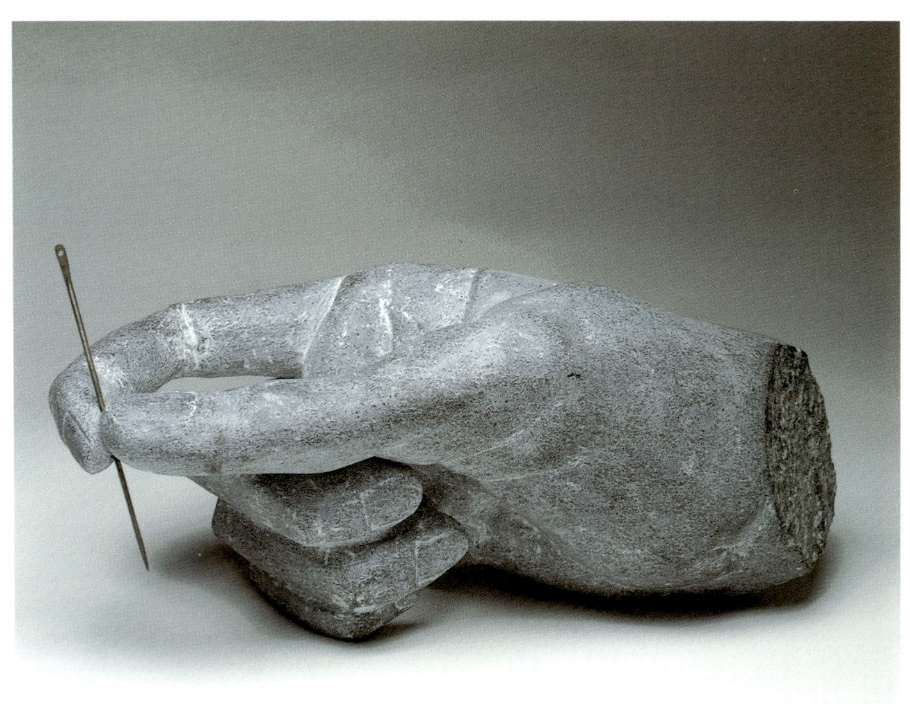

Untitled Hand 8
Soapstone, 10 x 19 x 9"

Laura
HUTTON

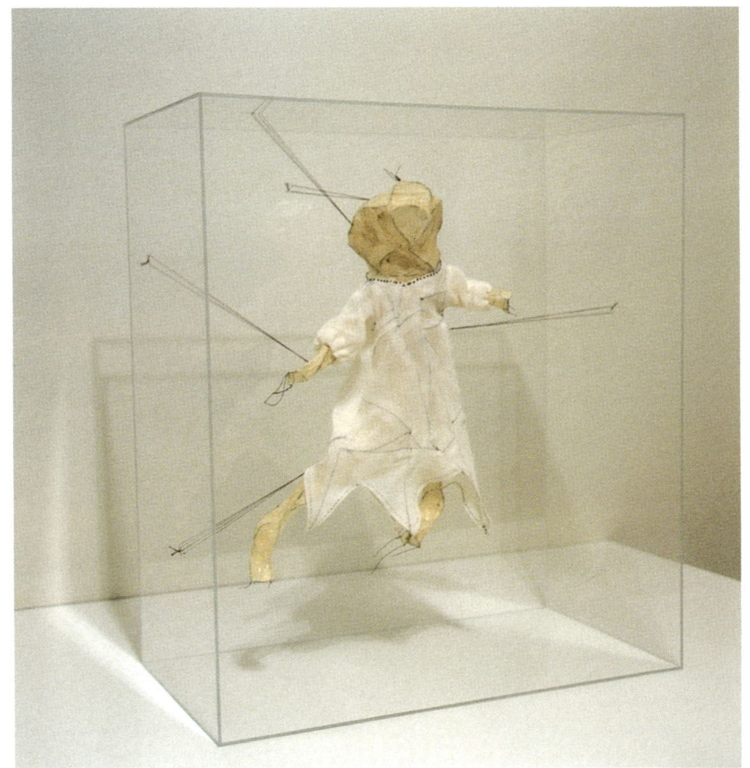

At what point does generation become deterioration, female become male, human become animal, entrapment become freedom, and comic become tragic?

My aim is to capture and suspend (literally) these moments and present them for your observation.

Specimen I
Copper, paper, glue, fabric, thread, and Plexiglas, 20 x 18 x 10 "

Hei Myung C. HYUN

Journey V
Acrylic on canvas, 48 x 36"

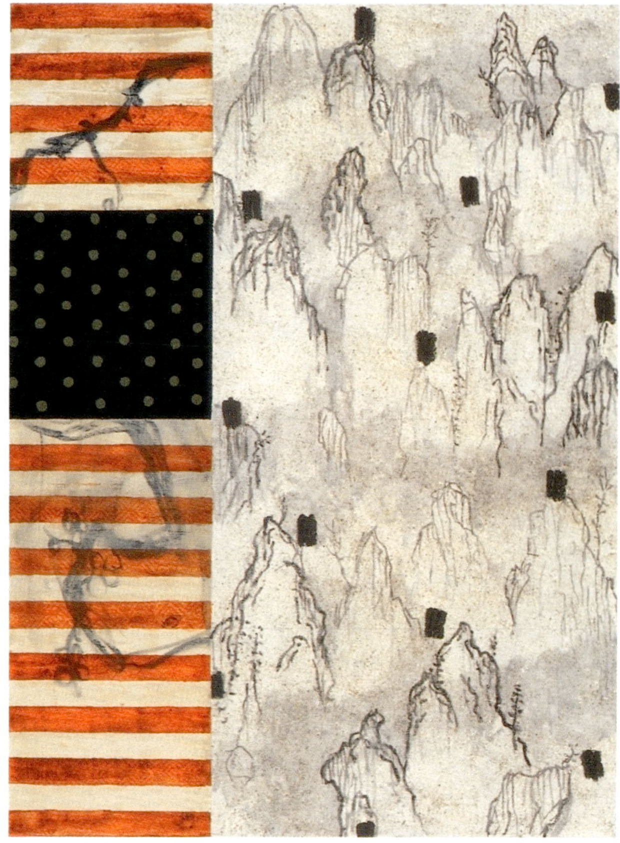

Judith Silverman JACOBSON

Crisis
Oil on paper, 48 x 42"
★ Berthe M. Goldberg
Memorial Award

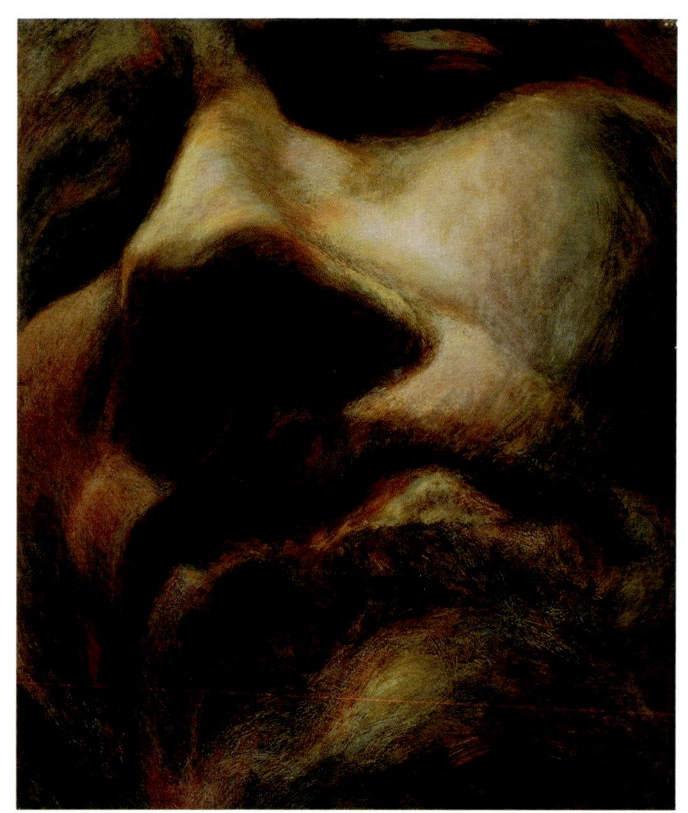

Nancy M.
JARAMILLO

Portrait of a Young Woman
Conté crayon on wood with
metal leaf, 17 x 13"
★ Honorable Mention

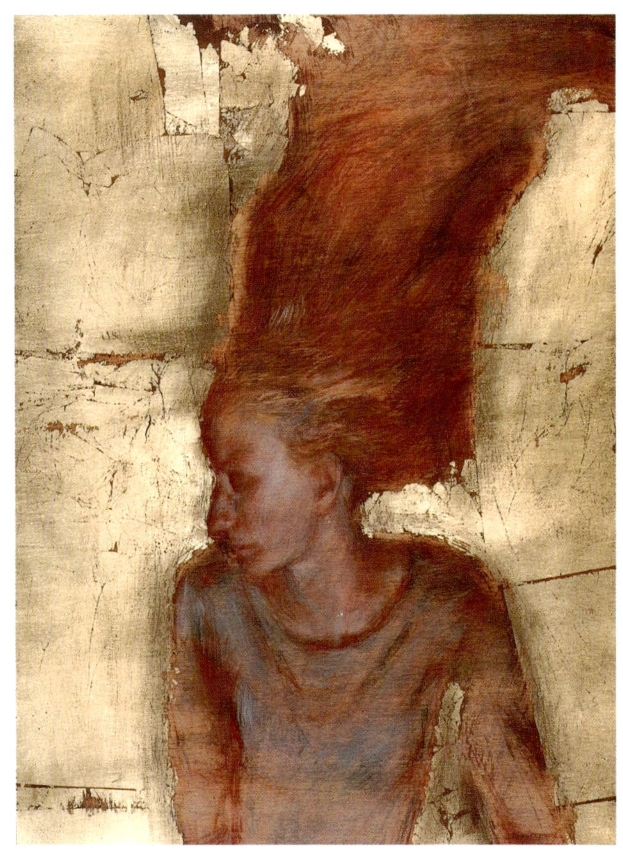

Richard J.
JOHNSON

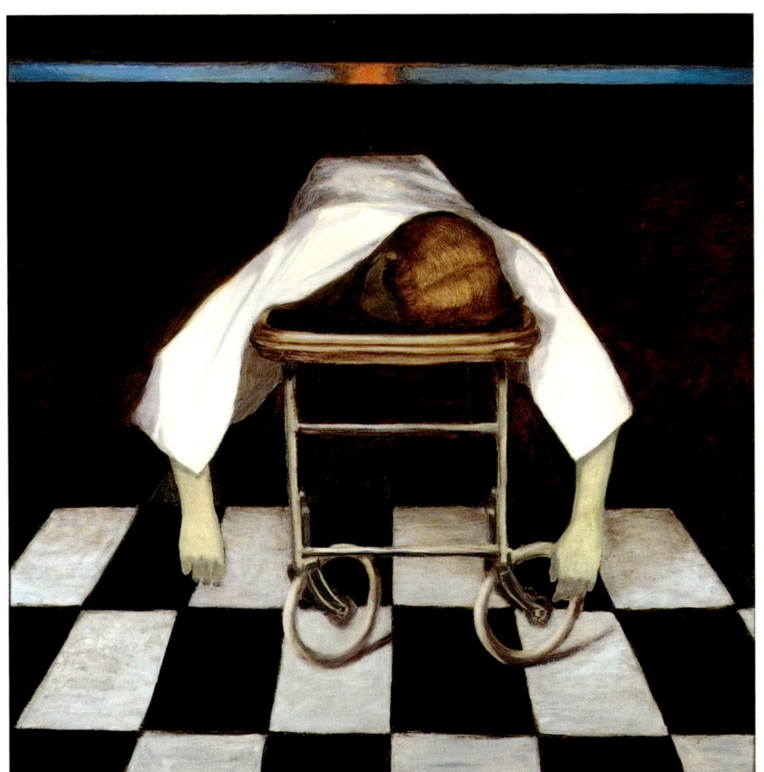

*"The fifth angel blew his trumpet,
and I saw a star fallen from heaven
to earth, and he was given the key of
the shaft of the bottomless pit; and
from the shaft rose smoke like the
smoke of a great furnace, and the
sun and the air were darkened…."*
Revelation 9:1-2

The Fifth Angel
Oil on panel, 48 x 48"

Jeff
KELLAR

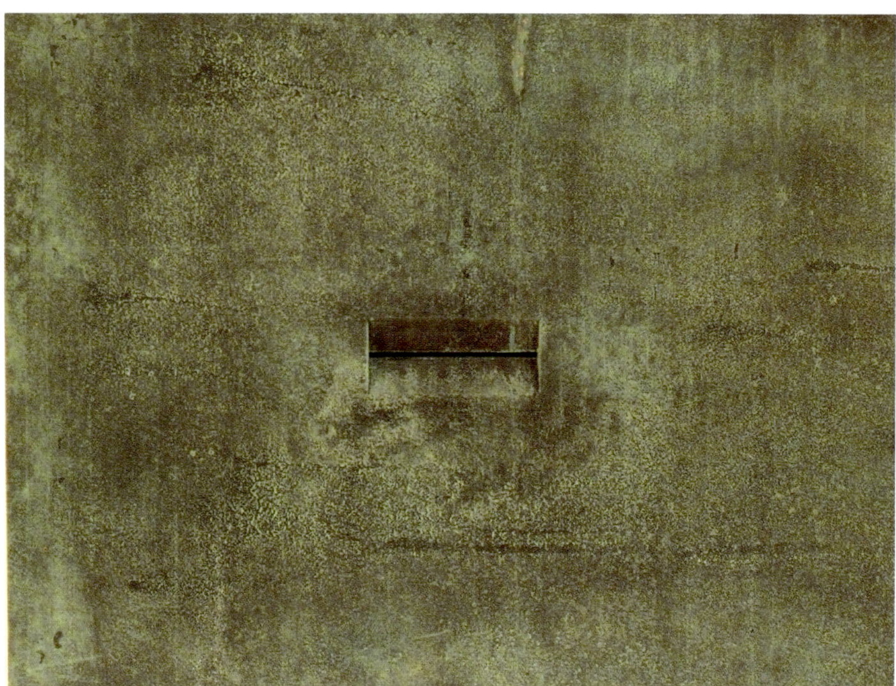

Misung
KIM

Walking into a corner

I exist, however, I am not existed.

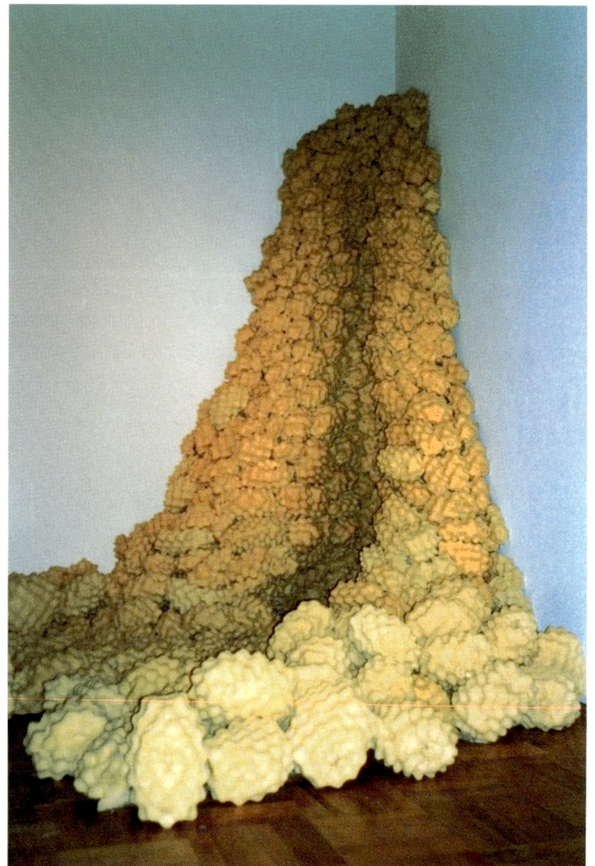

Untitled
Foam, 96 x 72 x 48"

Paul
KING

Waiting Woman
Oil on panel, 30 x 24"
★ Jack Bookbinder Memorial Award

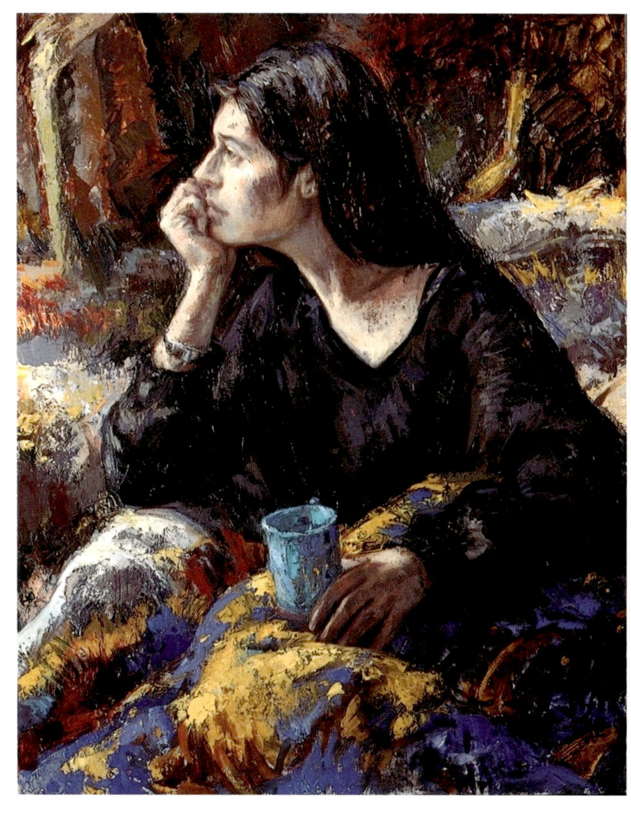

Tom
KING

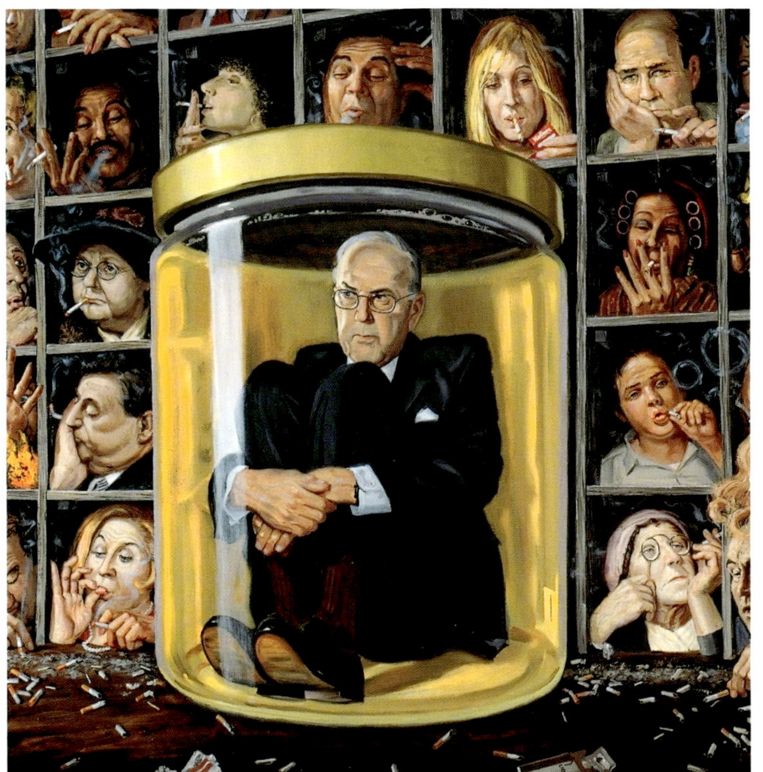

My paintings are social commentaries about prostitutional politics, the ever-lowering cultural and moral common denominators, over-population, pressure on endangered species, crime, and religious aspirations that seem to relegate our planet to a mere toilet stop on the way to heaven.

Rings, Lights & Haloes
Oil on canvas, 44 x 44"
★ Baker's Street Award

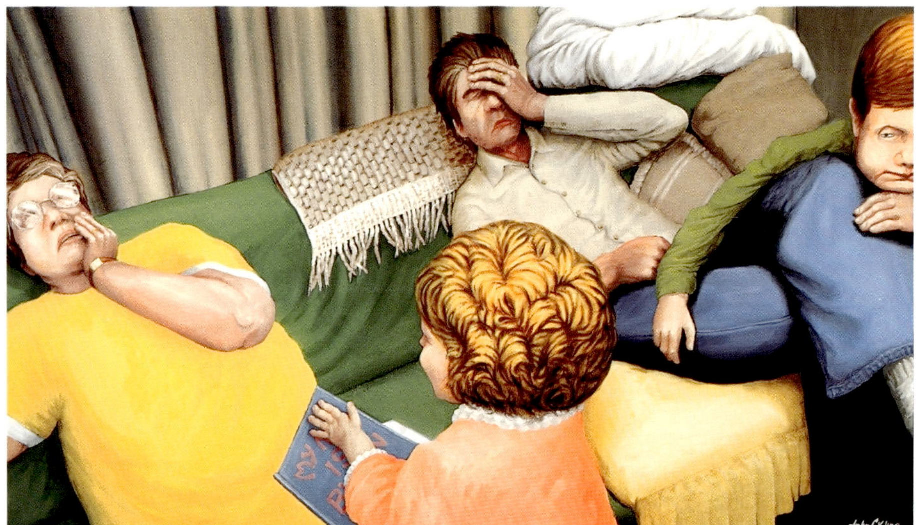

Tornado Alley
Oil on canvas,
40 x 70"

Rita
KLINGER

My work attempts to reveal the mysterious life of ordinary things. I work and rework an image from different views, in different media and colors until the actual image becomes secondary to its light, texture, and movement.

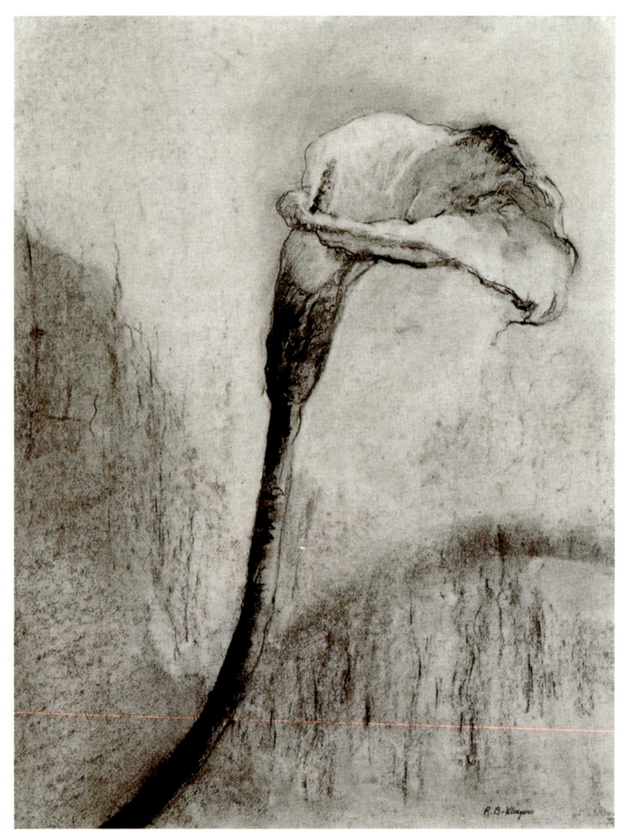

Dancer II
Charcoal, 32 1/2 x 27"
★ Mabel Wilson Woodrow Memorial Award

Black Spirit Vessel
Oil, 66 x 66″

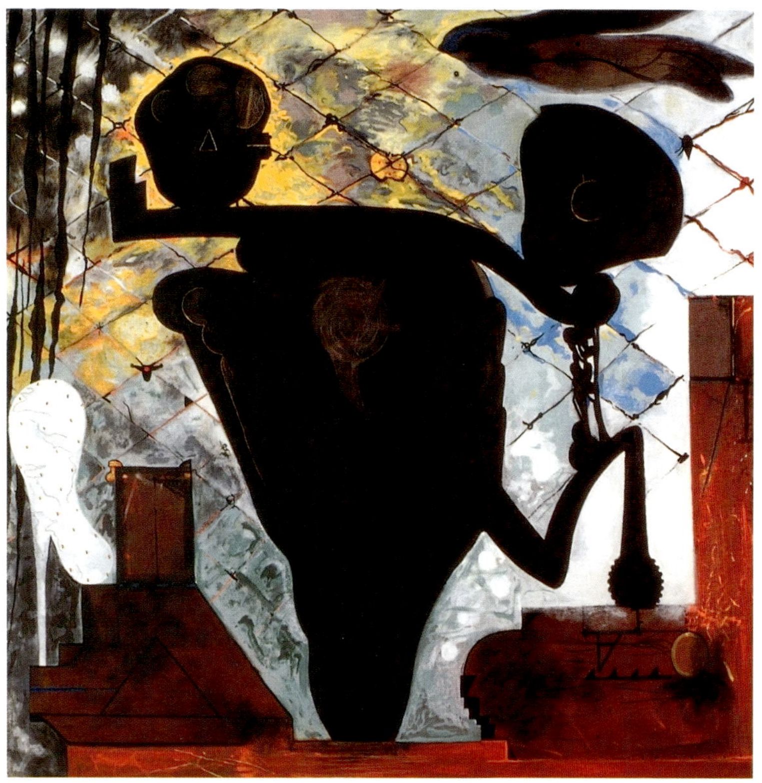

*Any additional talking, besides
what I have stated in my artwork, would not add anything
to it.*
*Therefore, I firmly believe that
it is the art critic's task to do
the talking, if there is anything
additional that needs to be said.*

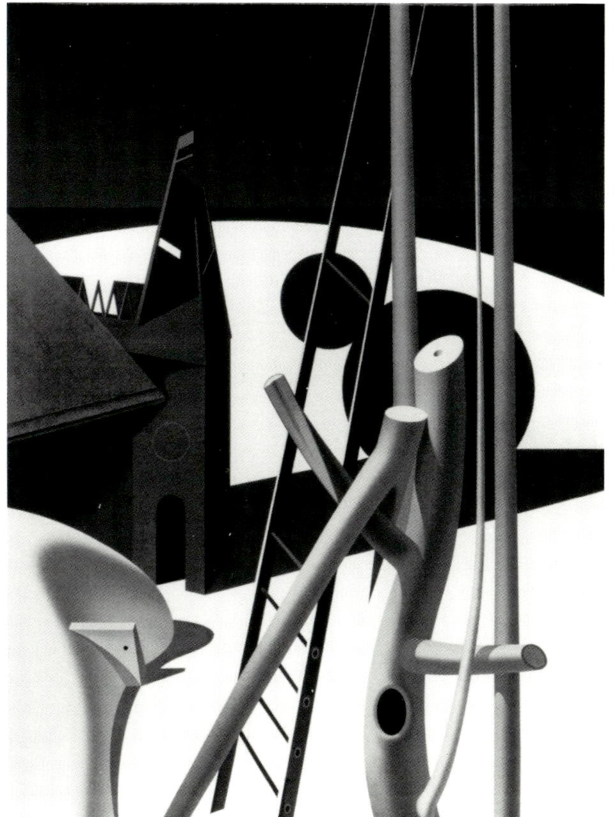

I Have Dreamed That a Steep Ladder
Iris print, 46 x 34″

Elaine M.
LISLE

*Most recently, I have been setting up
my easel in the Italian Market in South
Philadelphia. I am fascinated by the
diversity of architectural elements as
well as the colors, people, sounds, and
even the smells.*

Triple Play
Oil on canvas, 48 x 36"

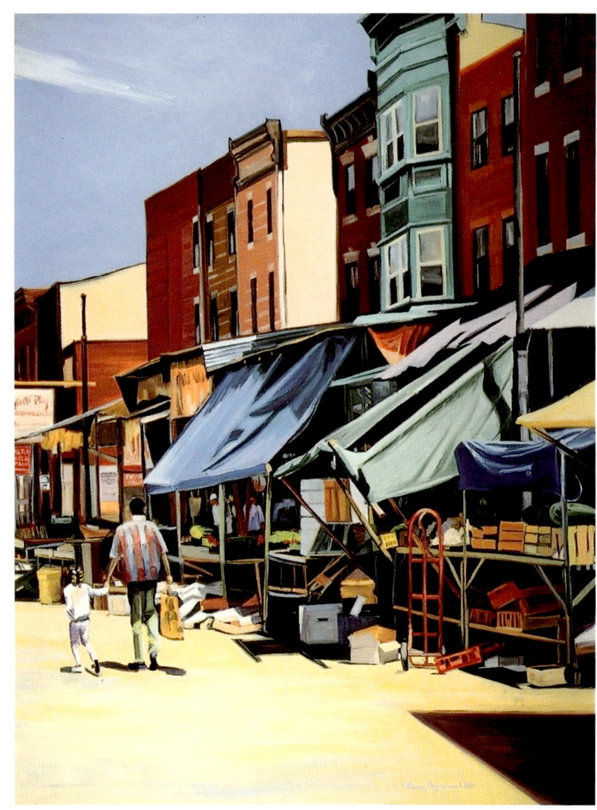

Patricia Hallock
LYNN

*This painting was done in memory
of my father shortly after his death.
I tried to capture the essence of the
man who raised seven children and
for forty years wrote a daily column
for* The Evening Bulletin.

My Father Remembered
Gouache on Strathmore paper,
27 x 22"

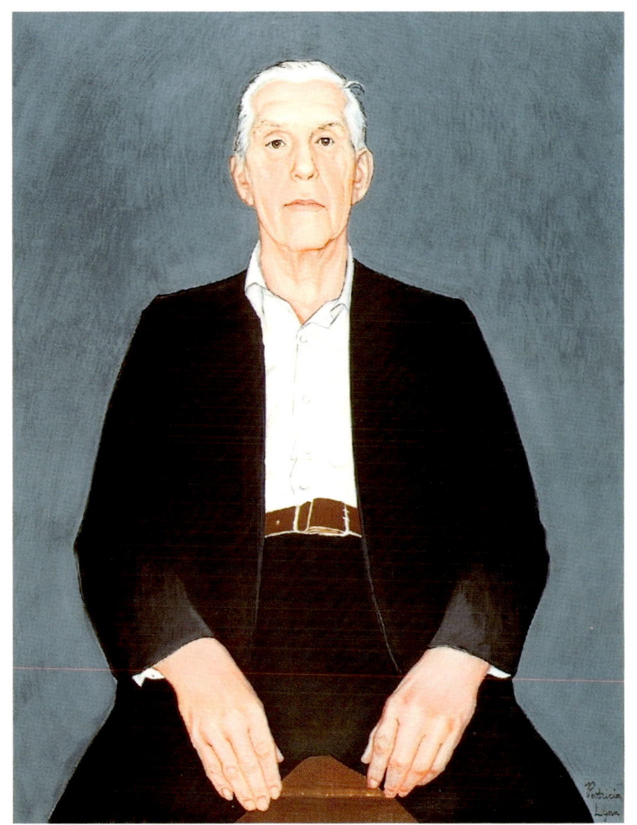

Douglas S.
MARTENSON

Starting to Draw
Oil, 46 x 78"

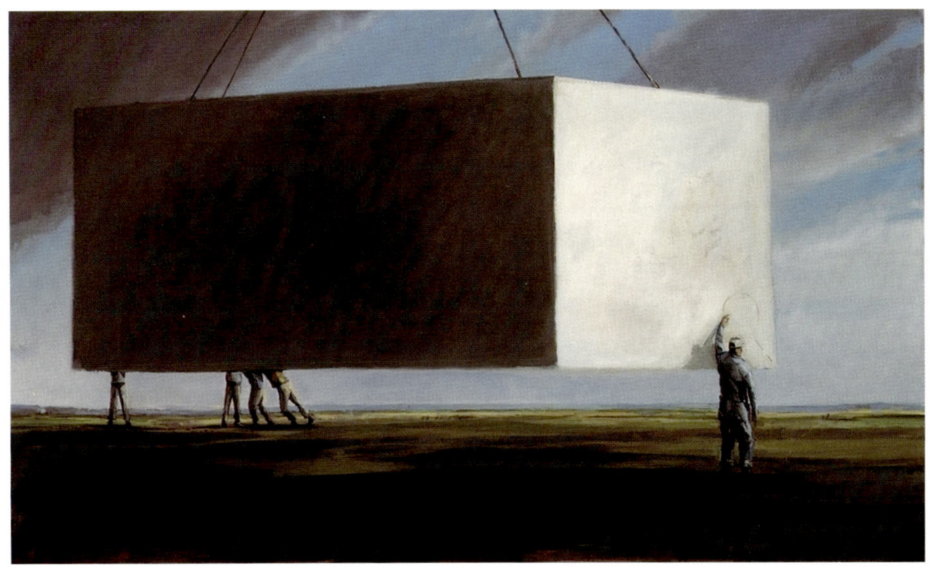

Lydia
MARTIN

For better or for worse, I paint to understand the world that surrounds me. Master painters knew that painting was a knowing, a seeing from within— outwards through the observing eye, recording all the many animated shapes and colors depicted in patterns of shadow and light.

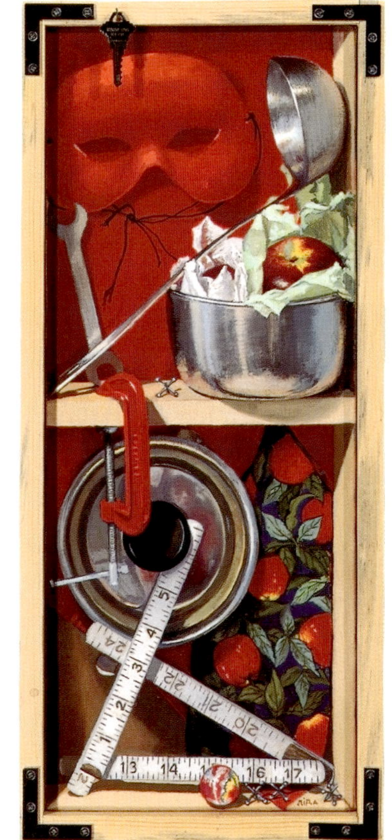

Scarlet and Stainless Steel
Oil on canvas, 24 x 8"

Joanna
MARTINEZ

*"It is within us that the
mysterious path leads.
Within us and nowhere
else is to be found the
eternity of all worlds,
the past and the future.
The external world is the
world of shadows and it
throws its shadow onto
the kingdom of light."*

— Novalis

Diptych—Moon Night
Acrylic and pastel on canvas,
64 x 75"
★ Honorable Mention

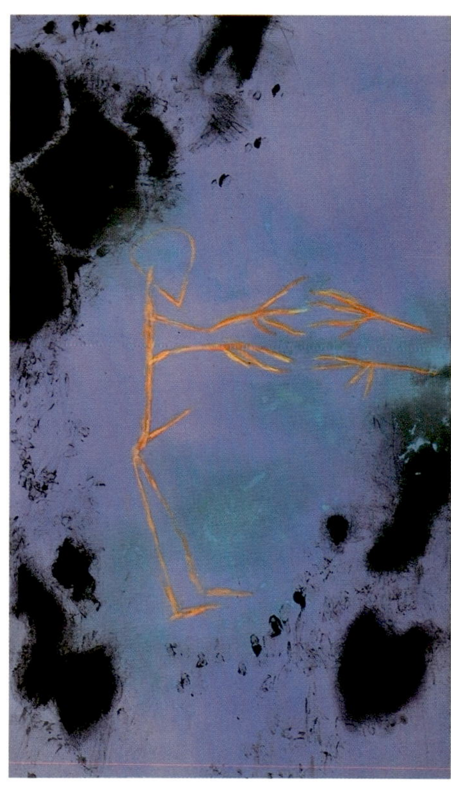

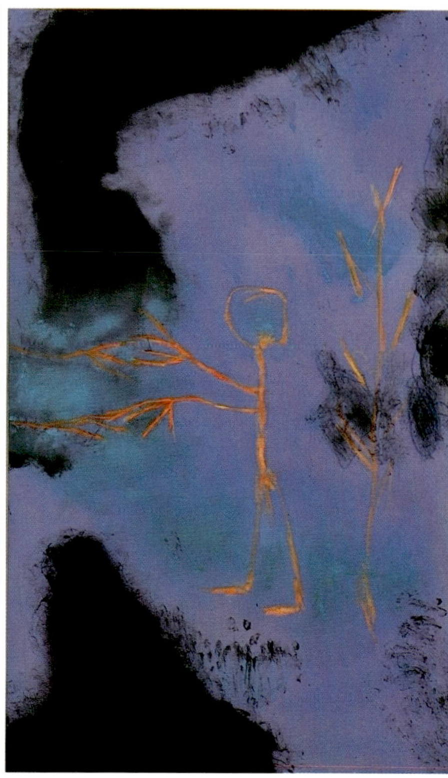

William R.
MARTONE

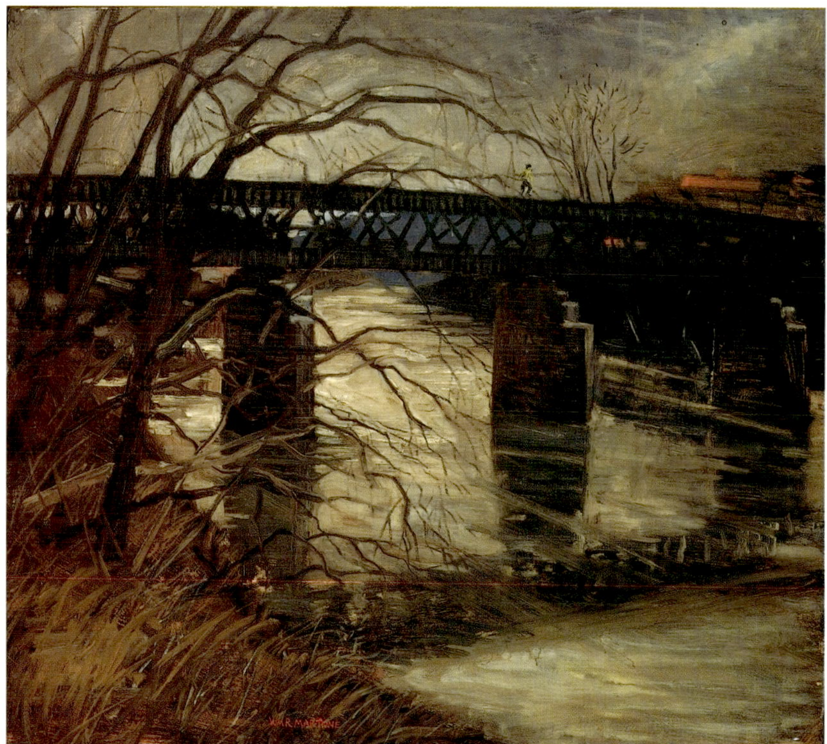

Winter Manayunk
Oil on linen, 28 x 34"

Eric
MCDADE

Each painting is subject to my excessive tendency to fetishize things (objects, images, etc.) until their usefulness has been expended or until I begin to take them for granted. Eventually, the charm is lost and I move on to the next item of interest.

Rose with Tape and Paint Smear
Oil on paper, 30 x 12"
★ Honorable Mention

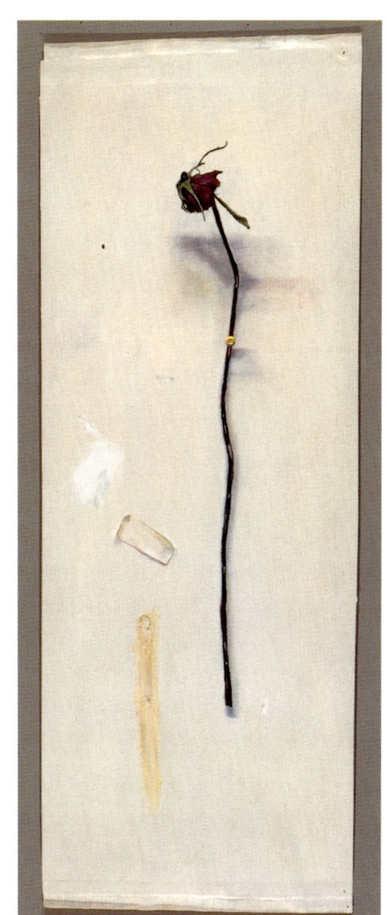

John T.
MEEHAN III

Stephanie and Clark
Oil on canvas,
12 x 16"

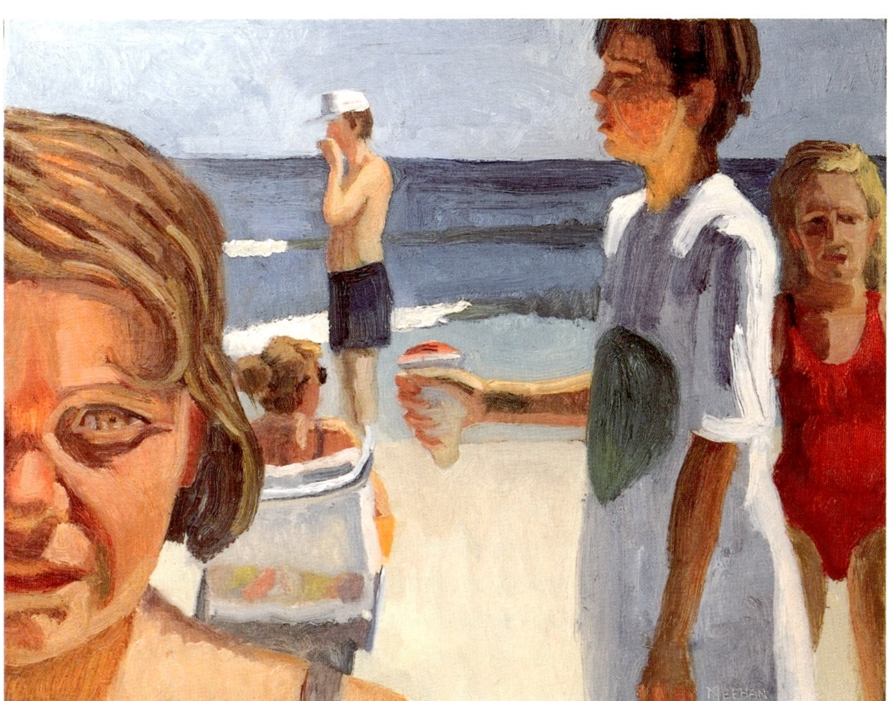

Elizabeth
MEYER

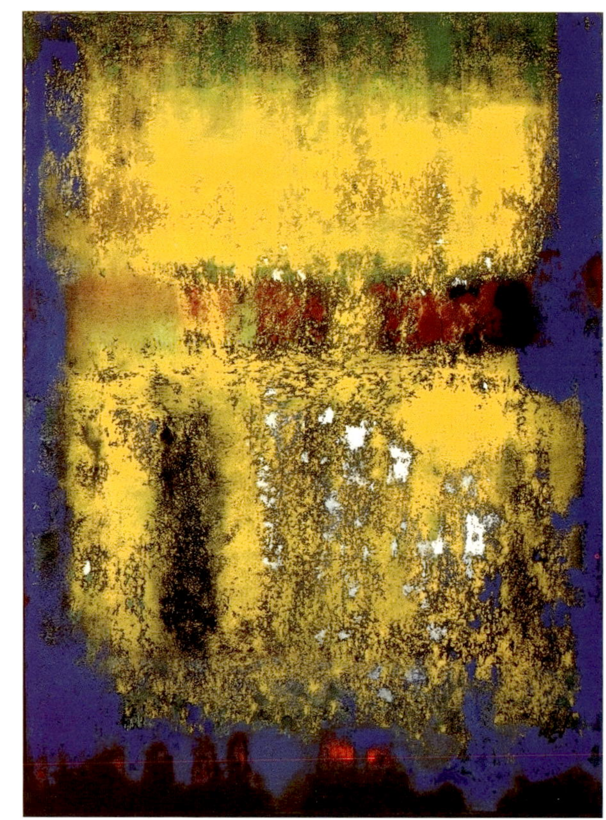

Night Window II
Pastel on Twin Rocker paper,
30 x 22"
Courtesy of Northwestern
Human Services

Ellen
MILLER

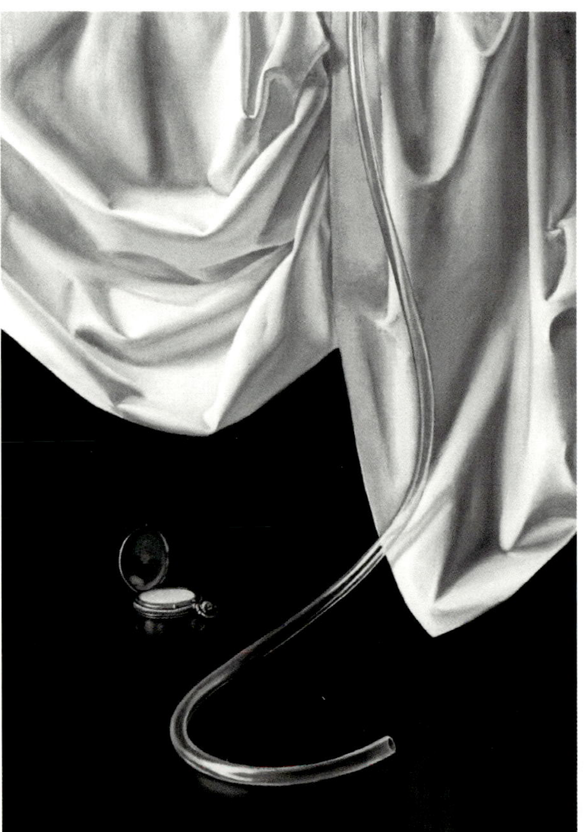

Dave 4
Oil on canvas, 28 x 20"

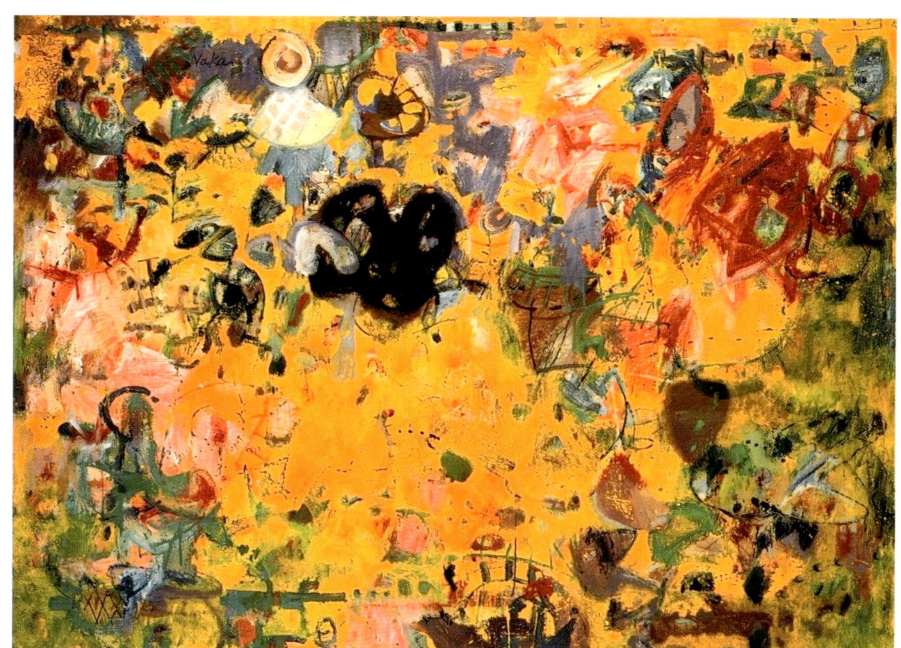

Whatever I can do today, I do it for today, not for tomorrow, nor for yester-day. The past comes in a moment. Tomorrow will be today. I just try to listen to the moment day after day.

Kamishibai
Oil on canvas, 48 x 68"

Regina
OVERATH

By the degeneration of film through process, I create printed images of rhythm and pattern.

Hoola Hoop Series II
Silkscreen on Plexiglas, detail 72 x 54"

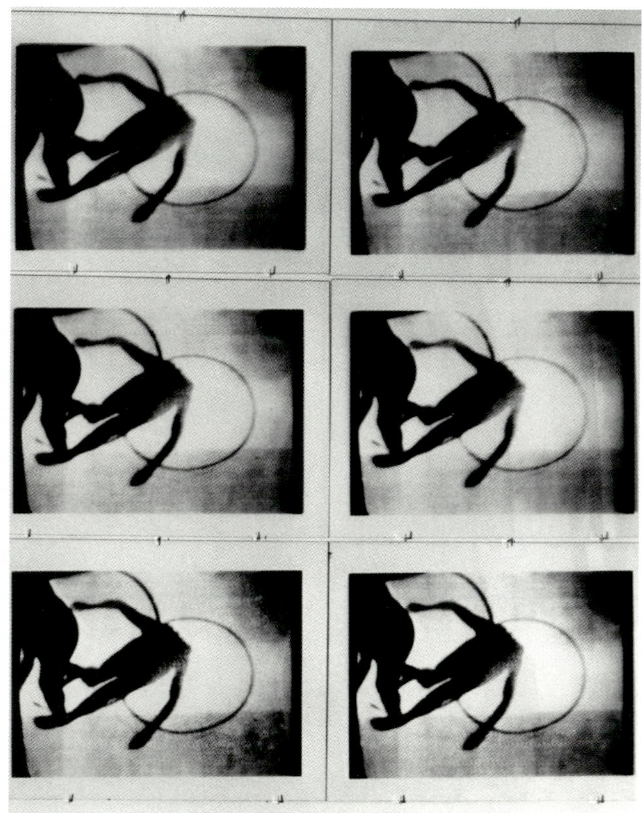

Katja
OXMAN

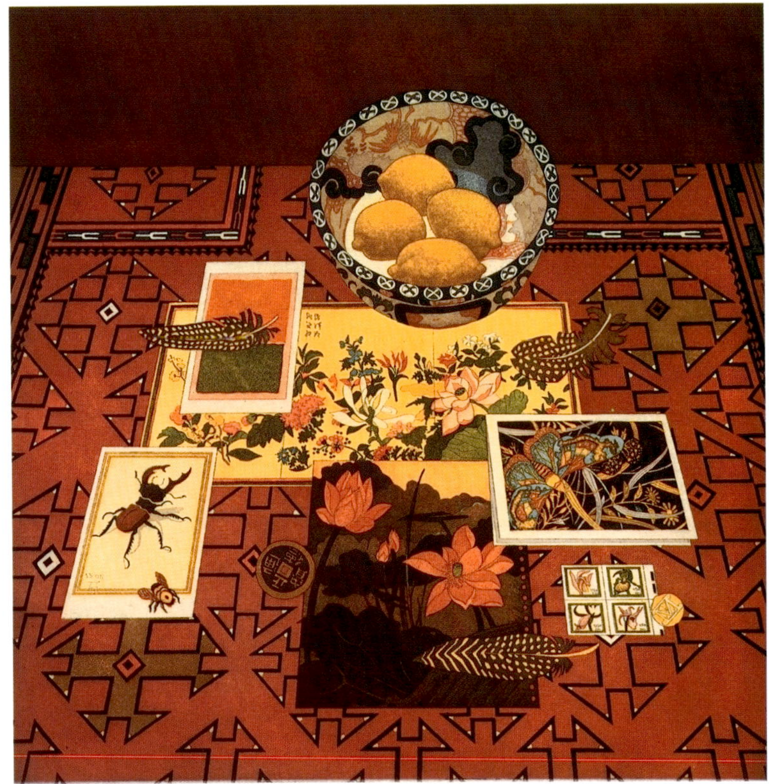

An Open Window
3-color etching and aquatint,
24 x 24"

Auseklis
OZOLS

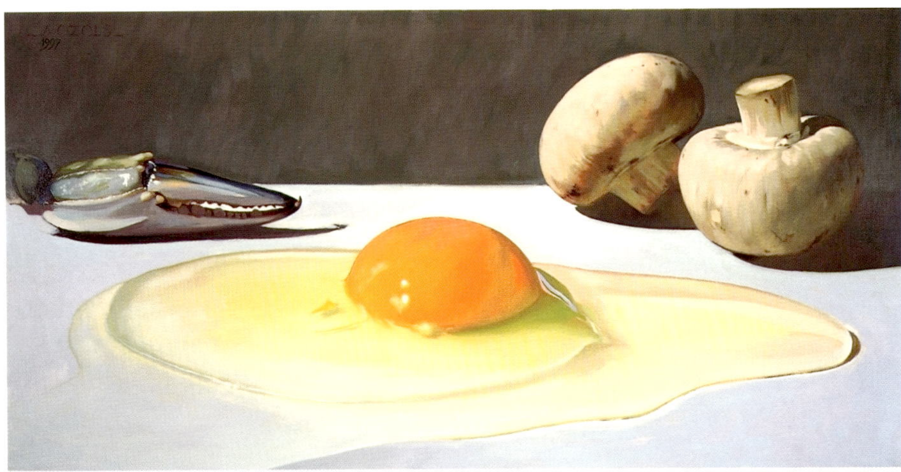

*Good Morning
America*
Oil on canvas,
24 x 48"
Collection of Mr.
and Mrs. James
Coleman, Jr.,
New Orleans, La.

THE TRIVIUM HELD IN THE "MEAN,"
THE GOLDEN ONE I MEAN,
To square the circle, thrice an angle,
double the cube, are keen.
Yet greater tasks await the heart that
yearns for sights unseen,
Much sacred labor love and hope, in
search of God's tontine.

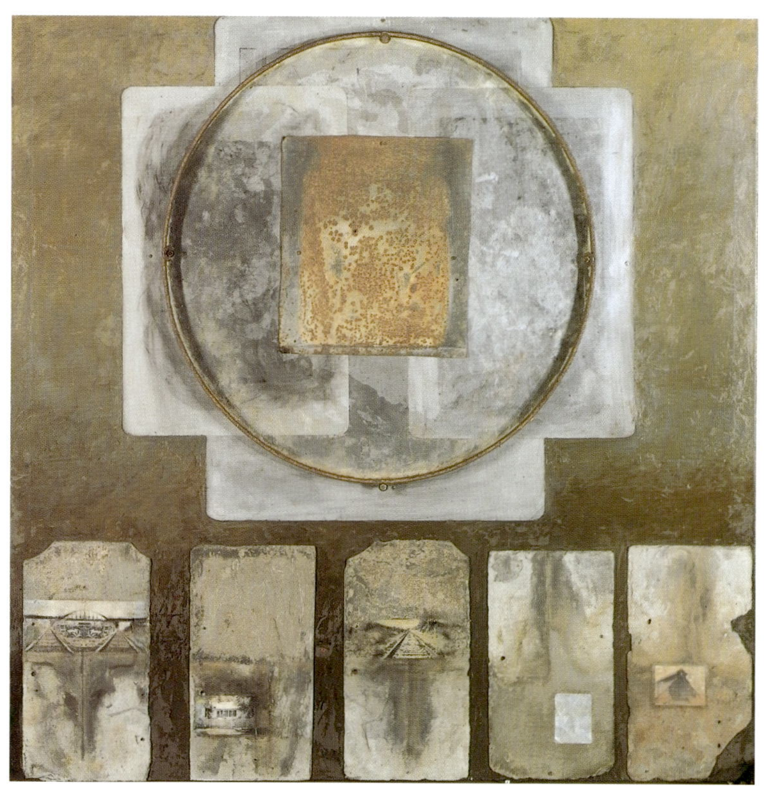

Non-Renewable Resource
Assemblage, 66 x 66"

Johanna M.
PETROPOULOS

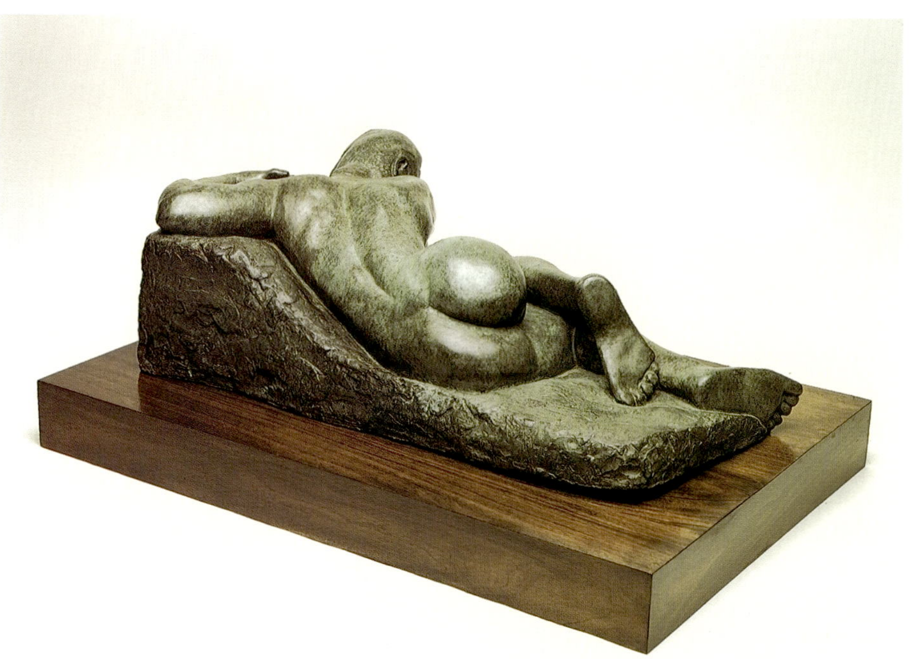

*Art is to be able to see,
combine creativity
with technical skills,
and bring out the
subconscious.*

Melancholia
Bronze, 11 ½ x 30 x 20"

Juan
PUNTES

*A new nomenclature
of discard
wearing Rosso's
substantive
shadows.*

Kabuki Home
Cardboard, tape, and tacks,
22 x 20 x 18"

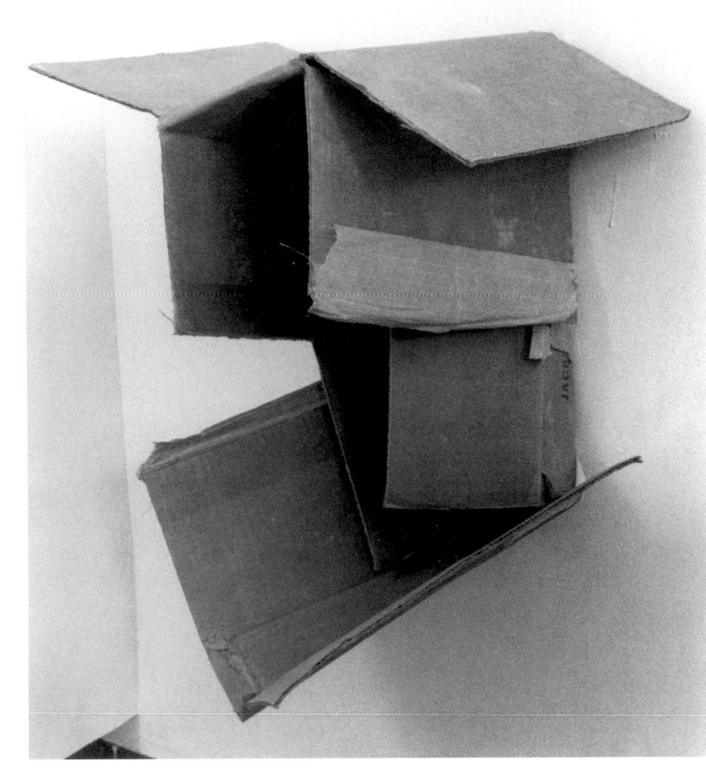

Douglas W.
RANDALL

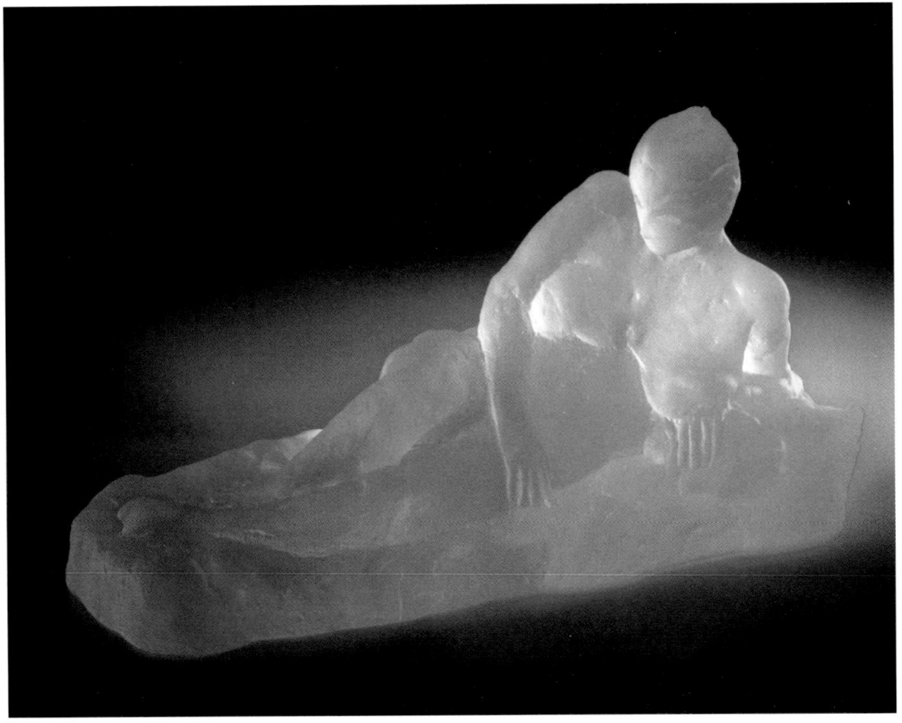

*I want my sculpture to
speak to the observer's body
as a feeling instead of a
narrative thought. I want
my glass to evoke a mystery
that brings the viewer into
the sculpture.*

Mother Earth
Glass, 3 x 6 x 13"

Easy Target
Oil on canvas, 30 x 34"

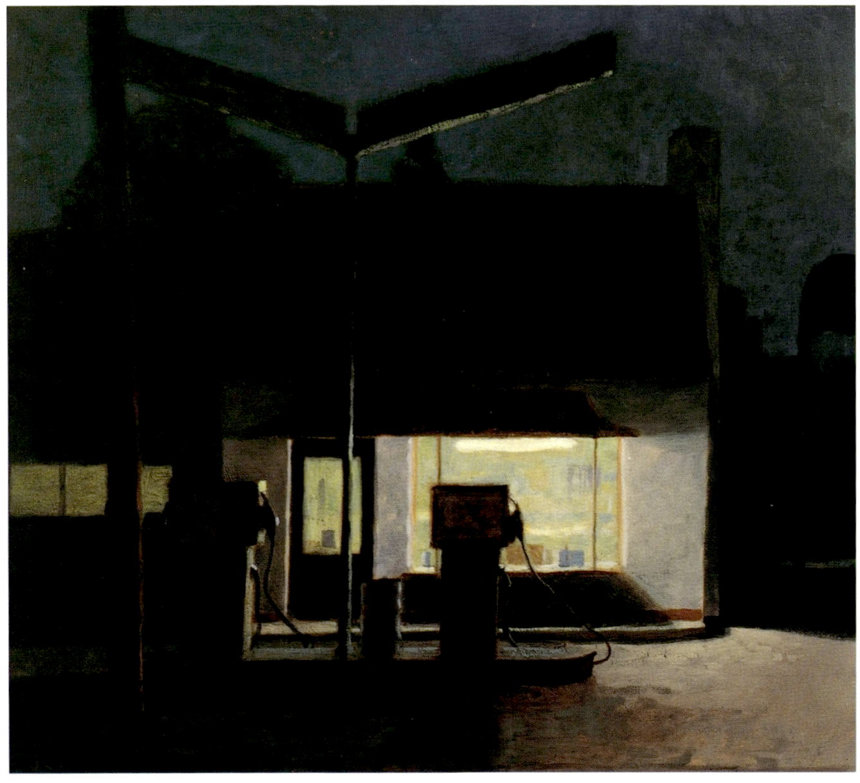

Huston
RIPLEY

Mourning Prayer
Acrylic on canvas, 78 x 96"

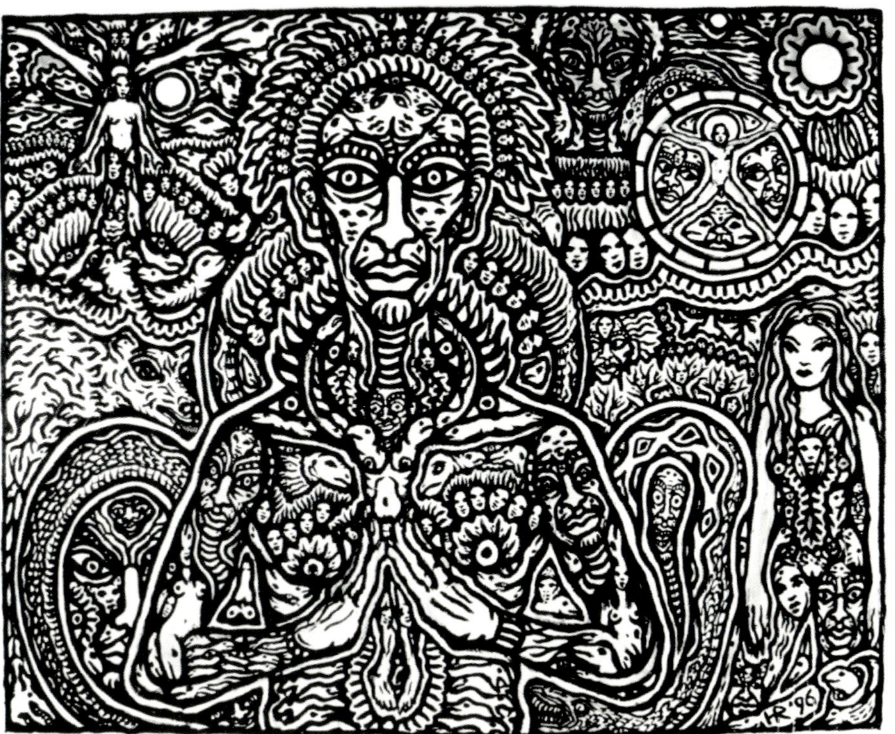

I like to think of my work as landscape profiles. I strive to interpret and express, through what are often imaginary land-scapes, the animated, psychological, and spiritual elements which are the essence of those landscapes.

Day's End
Monotype, 8 x 6"

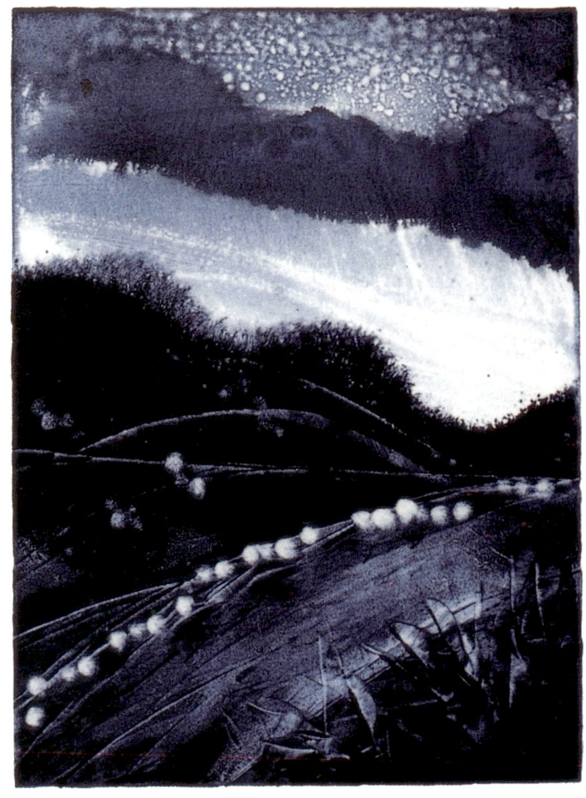

Untitled
Charcoal and pastel on
ragboard, 40 x 32"

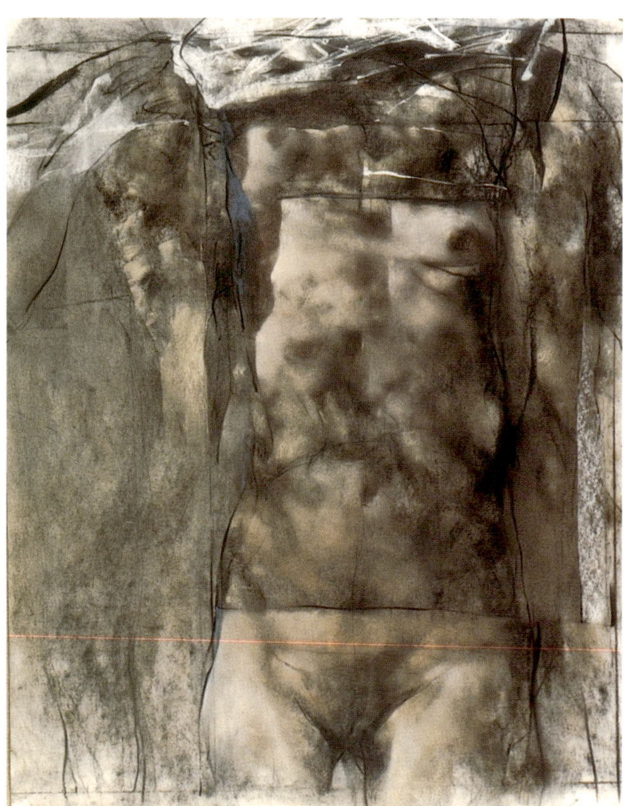

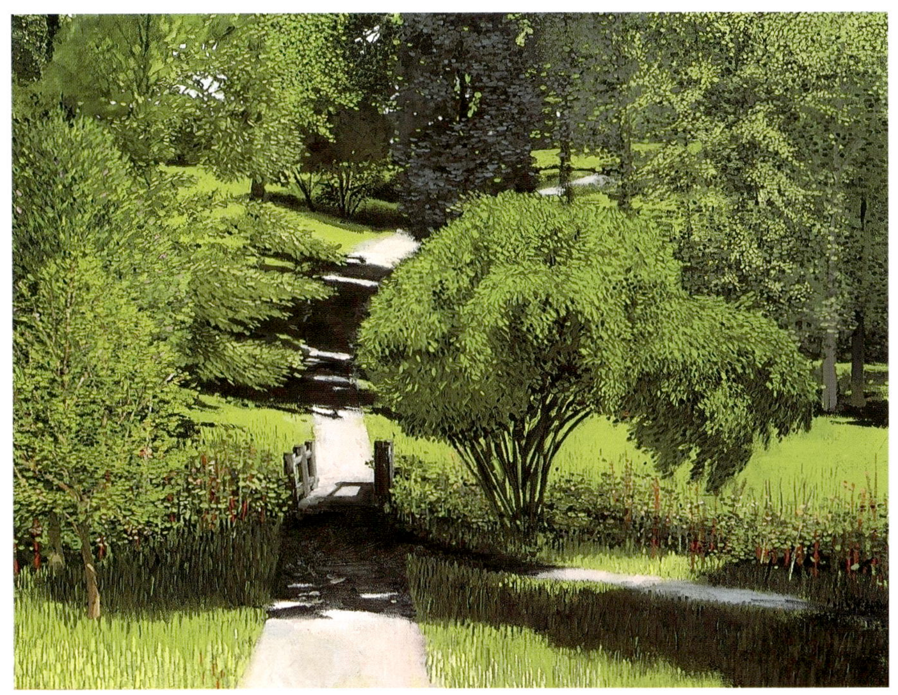

August — Lansdowne Valley
Oil on canvas, 18 x 24"

Bill
SCHMIDT

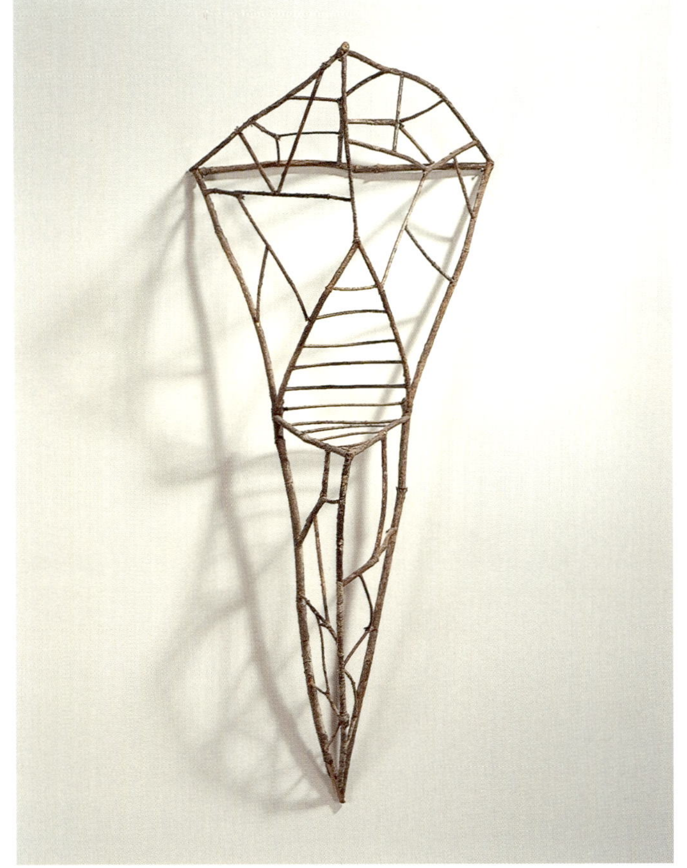

Snare
Twigs, 15 x 7 x 6"

"Walking Dunes," a.k.a. "Wow, Post-Contemporary Art"

My paintings are post-contem- porary because they are based on my own innate art sense, rather than on the dictates of the art world's bureaucratic elite. I see spatially, paint real- istically, fathom aesthetically.

The incredible complexity possible in realistic painting can never be fully exhausted.

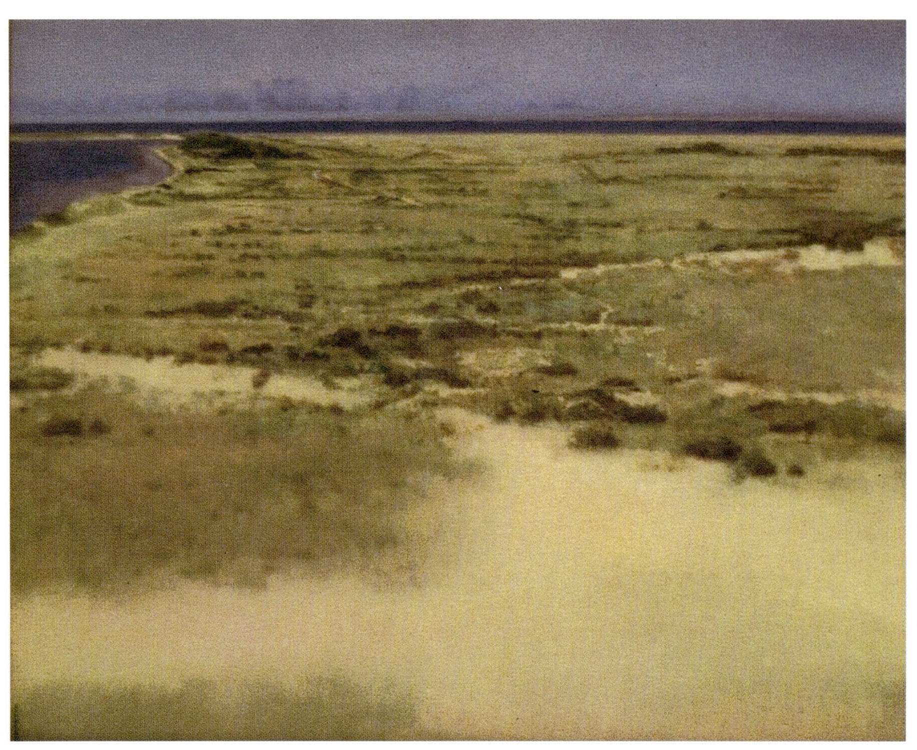

Walking Dunes
Oil on canvas, 23 x 30"

David
SHEVLINO

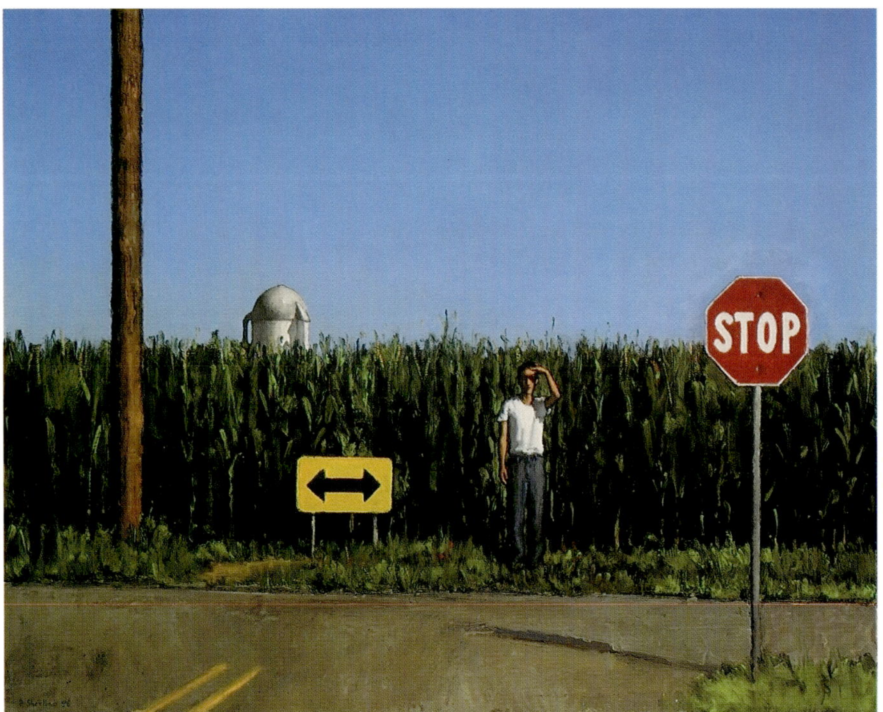

Field of Corn
Oil on panel, 24 x 30"

Jim
SIMMONS

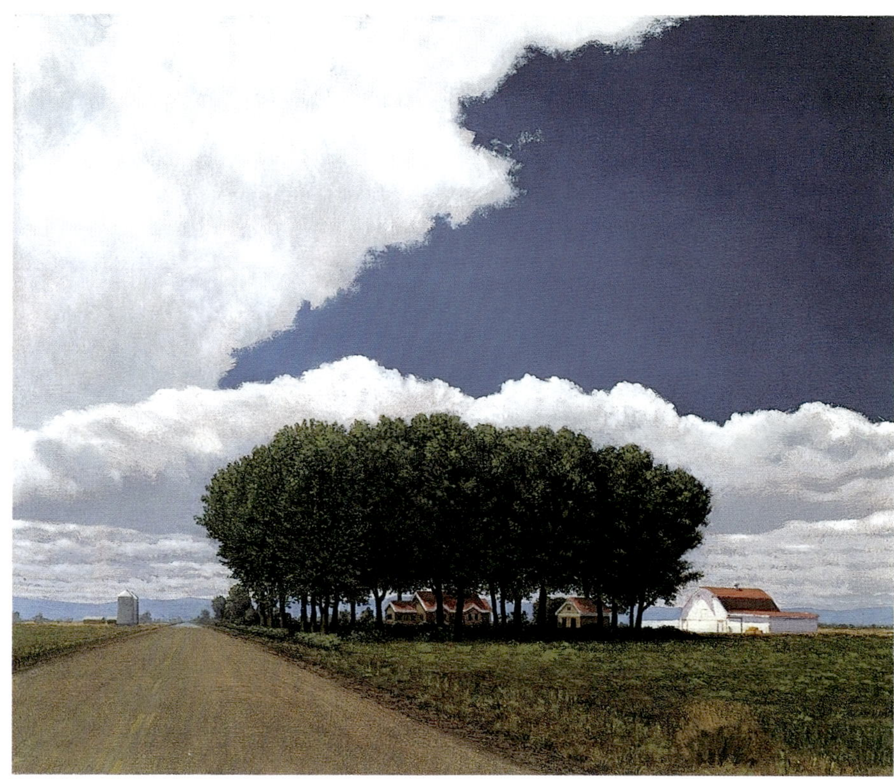

Ultramarine Sky, Alamosa
Oil, 19 ½ x 23 ½ ″

Joy
SMITH

Using these materials — paper, metal, plaster, wood, and light — I make three-dimensional images designed to evoke specific responses from the observer.

I try to demonstrate: contrasts, such as a ponderous shape made from delicate, translucent paper; illusions, such as that of metal or cement, through the surface treatment of the paper; and allusions — references to architecture, landscapes, and other parts of our environment, through the paper shapes and their placement.

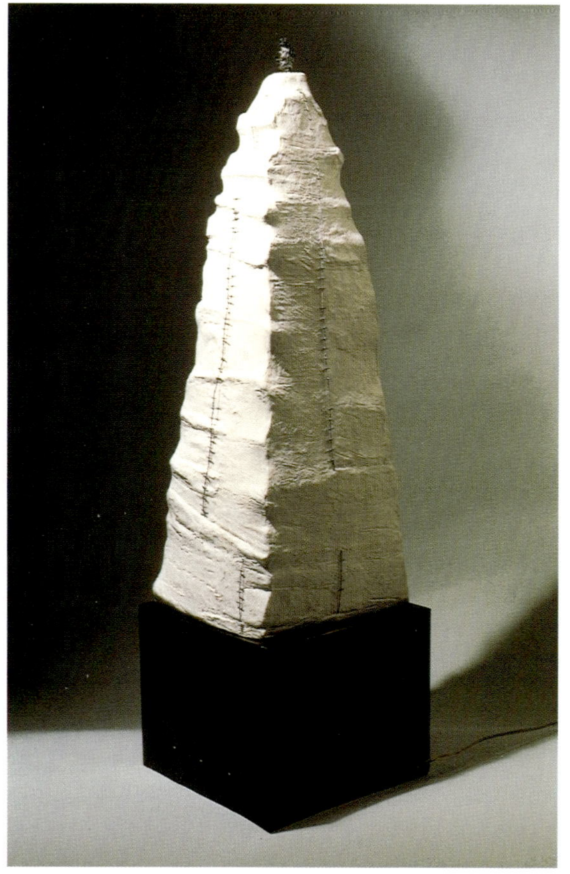

Ziggurat
Cast flax and metal,
20 x 10 x 10″

Mary
SPINELLI

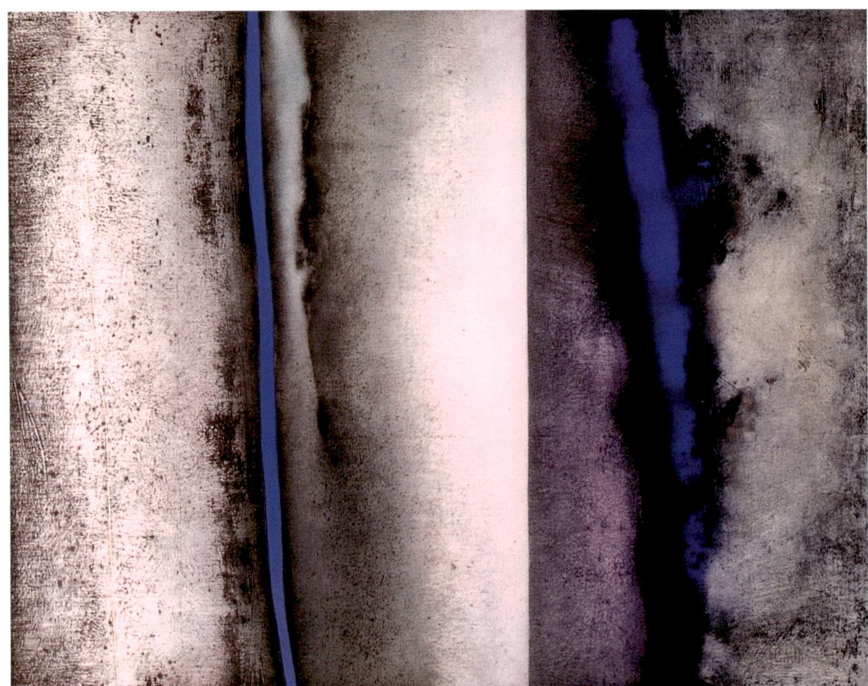

Untitled
Alkyd on museum board,
26 ³/₄ x 34 ¹/₄"

William
STEWART

Self-Portrait
Oil on canvas, 52 x 40"

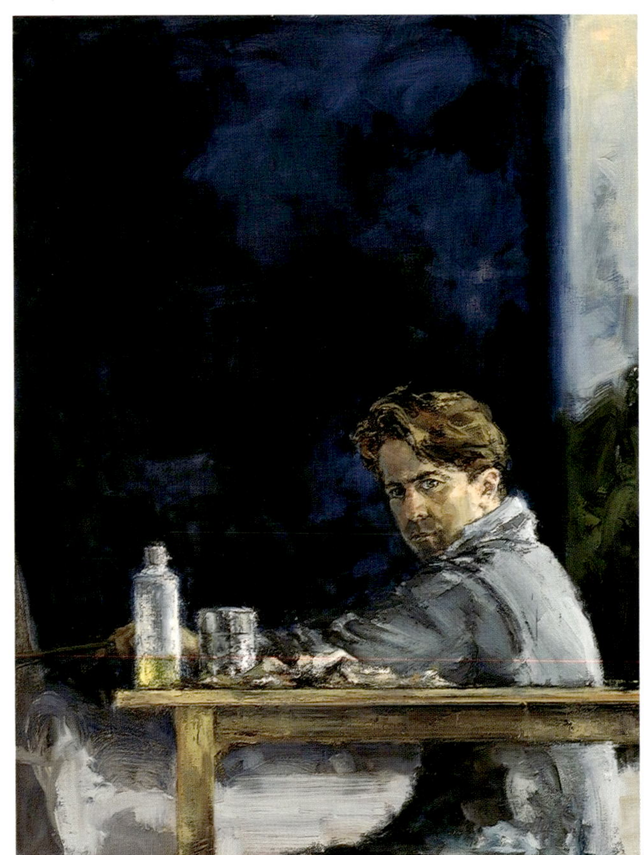

Rebecca Dvorin
STRONG

I live on an island, where I am inspired by the ever-changing light and atmospheric conditions to make paintings of pastoral landscapes, water views, and what might be called "skyscapes." This painting was made after a day of rain. The wind blew the clouds into huge masses, which were illuminated by the setting sun.

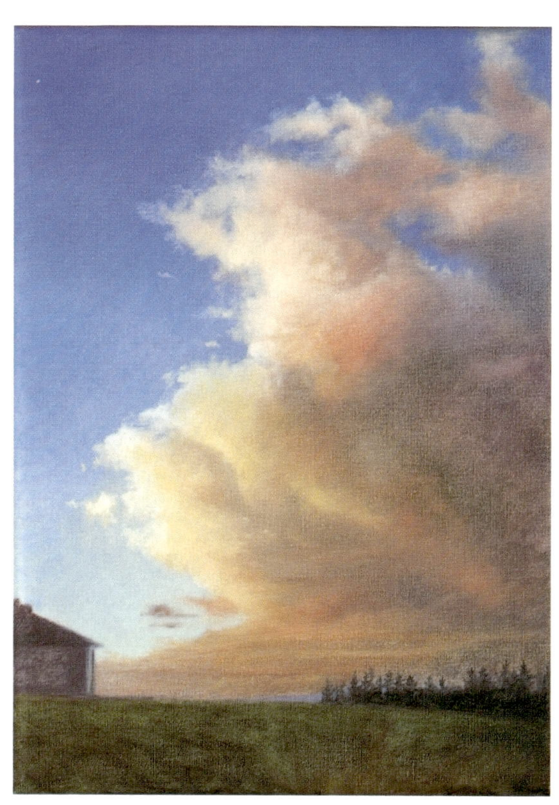

Big Cloud
Oil on canvas, 16 x 12"

Nancy H.
TAPLIN

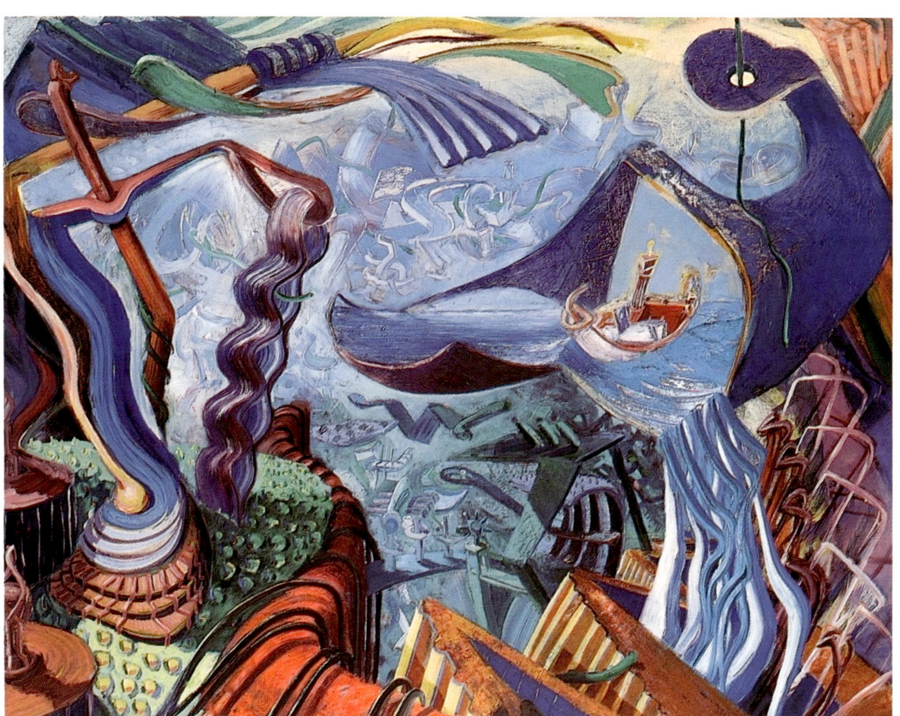

Tipping the Scales
Oil on panel,
48 x 62"

William G. TEODECKI

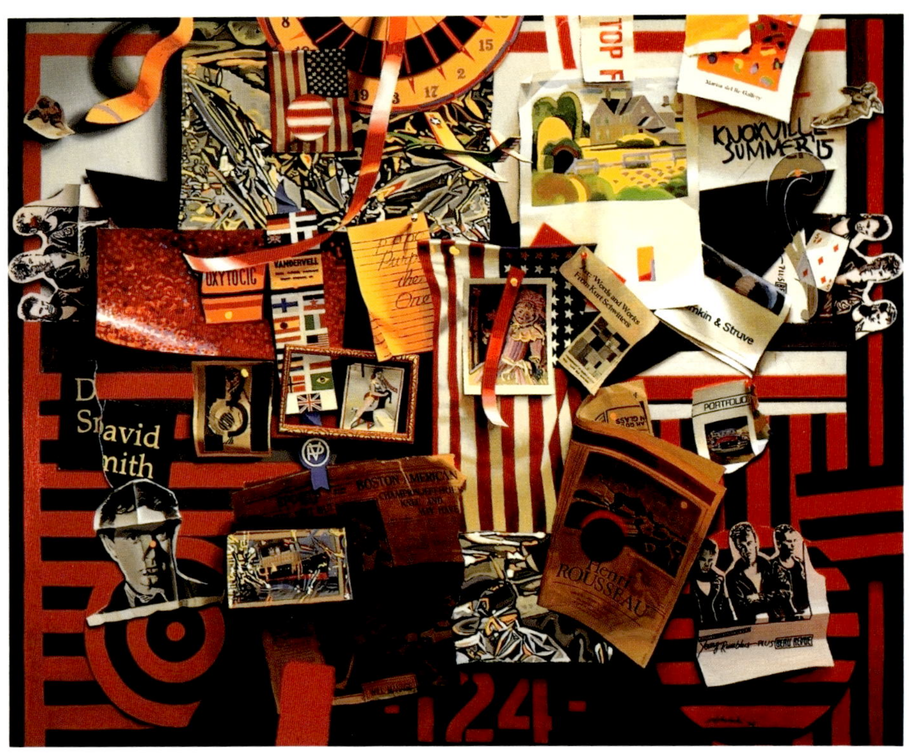

Purple is The One
Oil on canvas, 46 x 60"

Glenn THOMAS

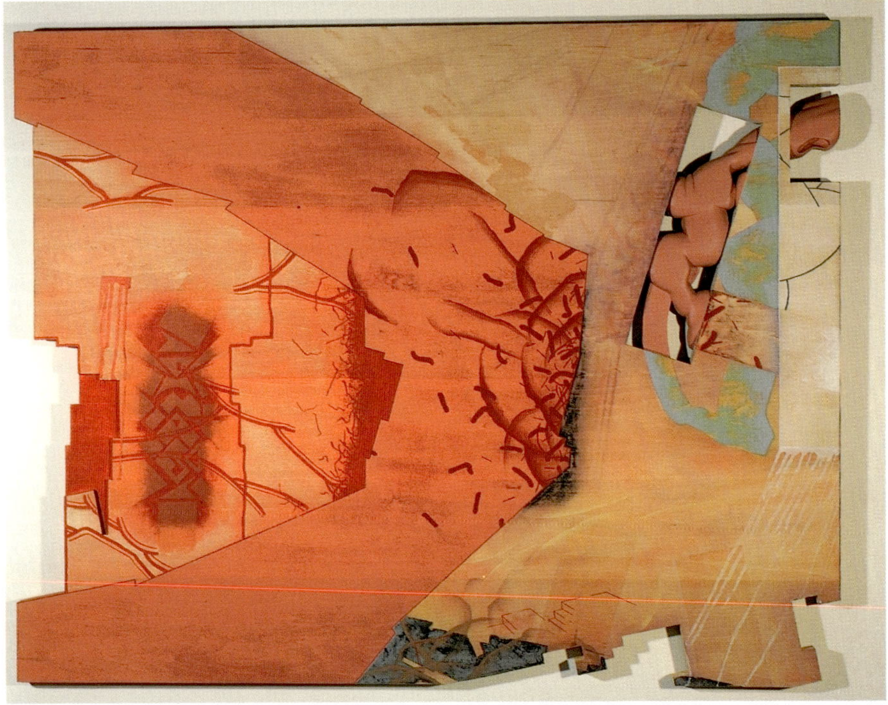

Glenn Thomas, painter, sculptor, and printmaker, was born on July 25, 1944 in Newark, New Jersey. He has been living and working in Amsterdam, Holland since 1970.

Cadiz
Acrylic on limewood panel,
39 $\frac{1}{2}$ x 51 $\frac{3}{4}$ x 2 $\frac{1}{2}$ "

Too Late Now
Oil on canvas,
34 x 54"

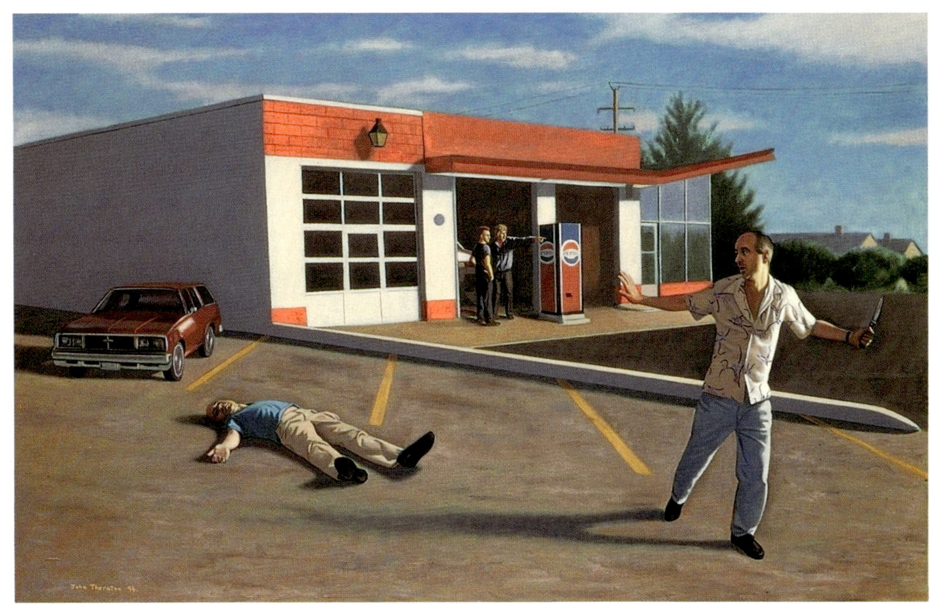

Young Girl
Painted cherry,
19½ x 9½ x 17"

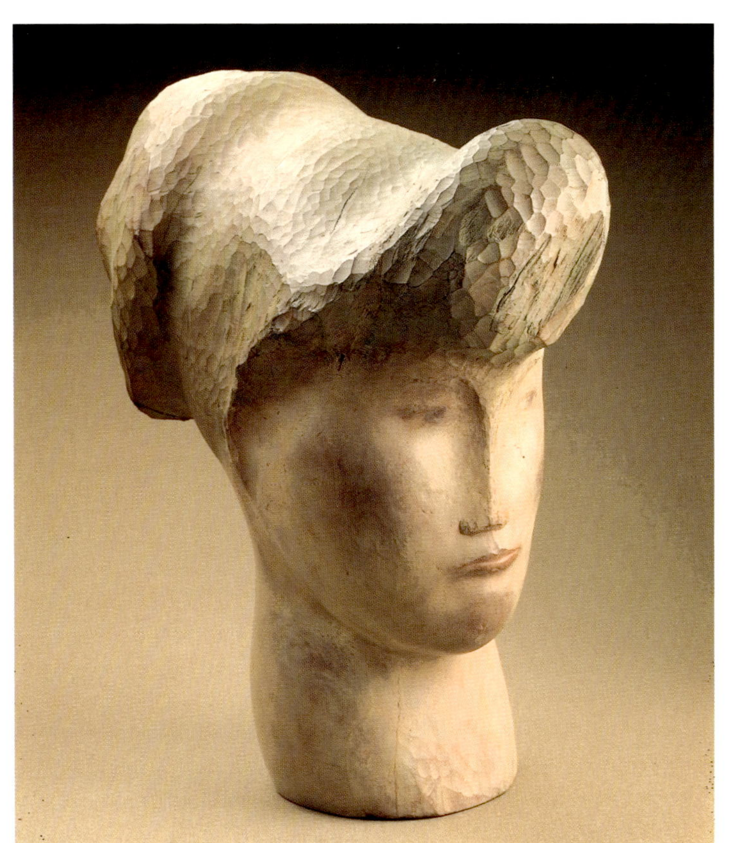

Susan
ULLMANN

Indigo Heights
Oil on paper, 29 ³/₄ x 22″

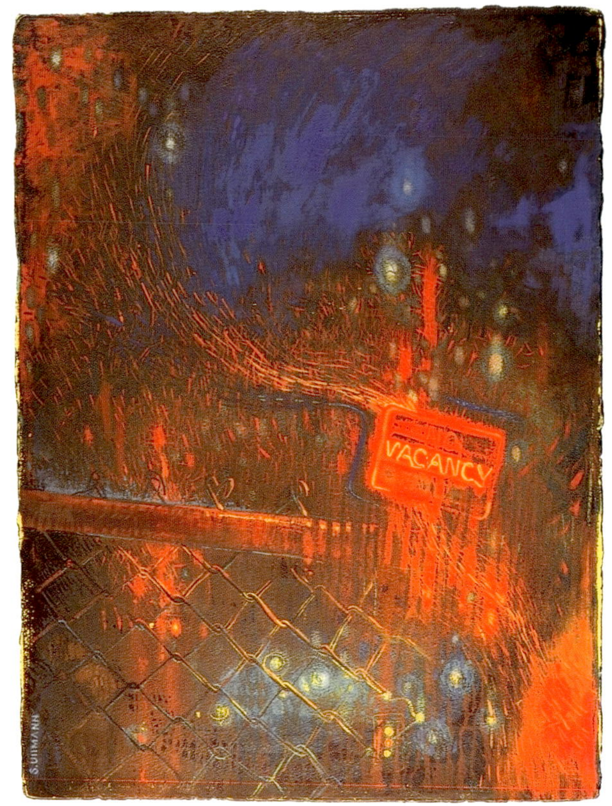

Mark
WALLISON

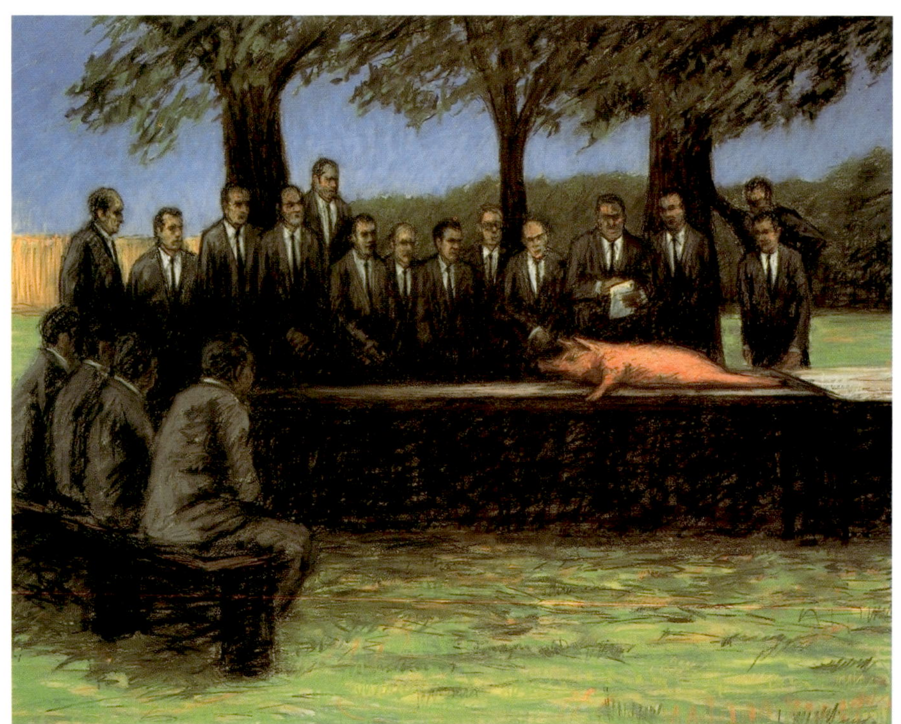

The Meeting
Pastel on paper, 26 x 33″

Gary
WEISMAN

Without
Bronze, 23 x 5 x 5"

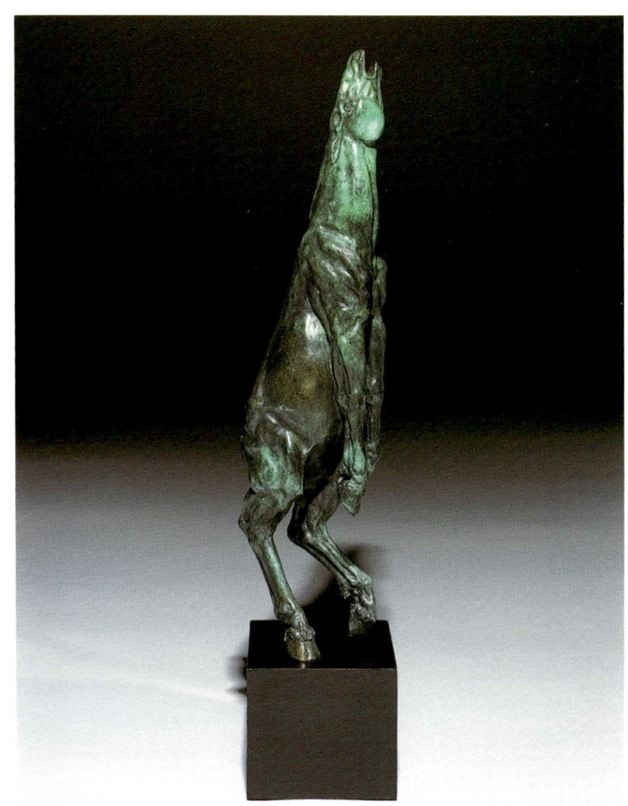

Scott
WHEELOCK

The Air
Bronze, 60 x 12 x 12"

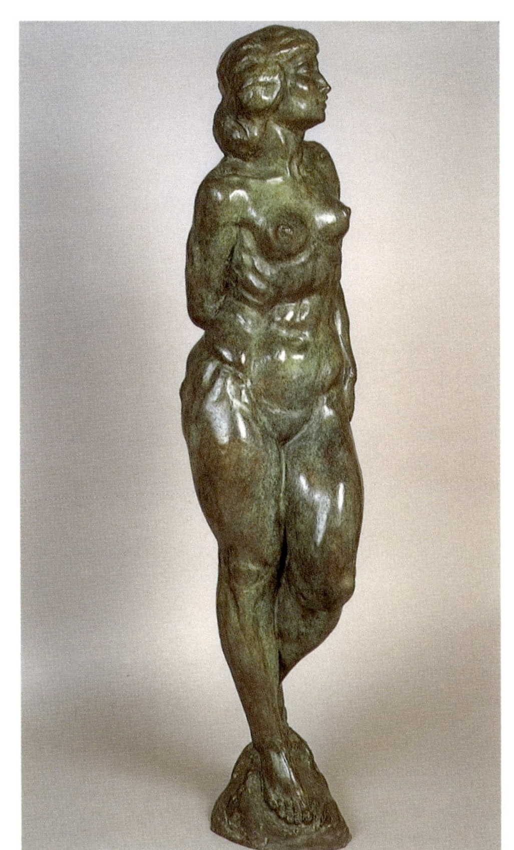

Elizabeth
WILSON

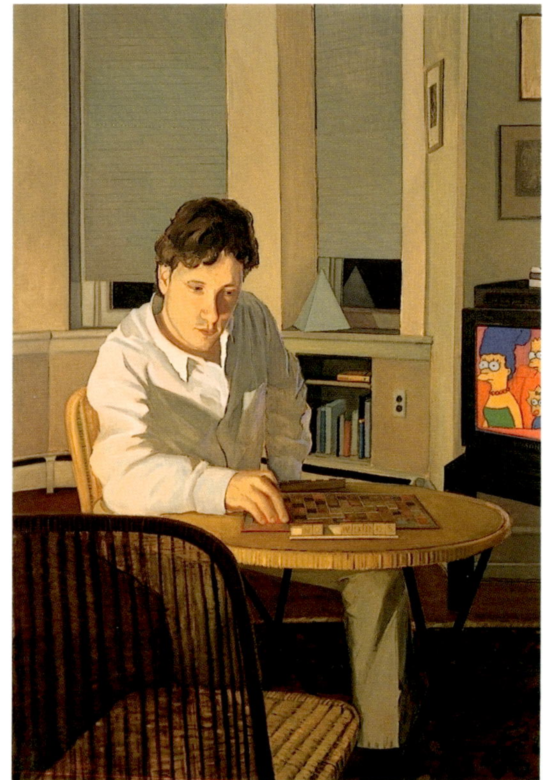

Scrabble
Oil on linen, 72 x 50"

Harriet
ZEITLIN

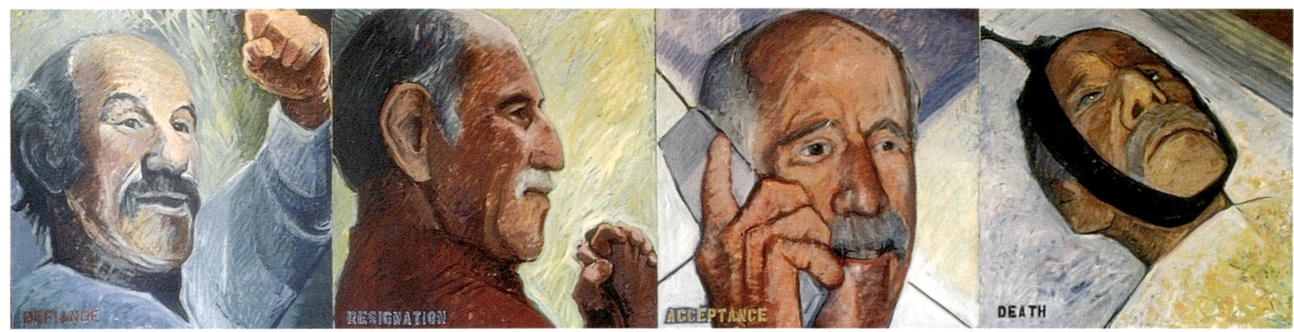

Terminal Illness
Acrylic on canvas, 54 x 216"

*"Terminal Illness" is a portrait of my husband,
David Zeitlin, who died of stomach cancer.
I painted it in tribute to his courage and dignity.*

JURIED WORKS

Courtesy of the artists, unless otherwise credited
Dimensions are in inches: height precedes width precedes depth

1. **Lorraine Alexander**
Xian: Market
Mixed collage and oil paint,
30 x 40"
Private collection

2. **Eleanor Allen**
Jessica
Oil on linen, 42 x 32"

3. **Jock Anderson**
The Homecoming
Oil on linen, 40 x 50"

4. **Dennis Aufiery**
Balseros, Havana
Oil on canvas, 65 x 80"

5. **Bethany Anne Ayres**
Pinwheel
Charcoal and graphite,
70 x 45"

6. **Jennifer Baker**
Warehouse Burning, American Street
Oil on mylar, 39 x 26"

7. **Joseph Barbieri**
Commission
Oil on canvas, 19 x 10"

8. **Robert Beck**
Light Duty
Oil on panel, 24 x 30"

9. **Lee F. Behl**
Brother & Sister
Oil, 72 x 48"
Collection of Ms. Richelle Kaufman

10. **Frank Bender**
Lest We Forget
Bronze, 22 1/2 x 10 x 12"

11. **Stanley Bielen**
Frustration of Faith
Oil on linen, 24 x 30"
Collection of Jane Barry and Dr. Patrick O'Kane

12. **Brett Bigbee**
Toy Truck
Oil on canvas, 43 15/16 x 35 3/16"
★ Catherine Gibbons Granger Award

13. **Heiko Blankenstein**
Pantheon
Concrete and steel,
30 x 50 x 50"
★ Lucy Glick Memorial Award and Mabel Wilson Woodrow Memorial Award

14. **Rachel Bliss**
Miss Lou
Oil and acrylic on canvas,
18 x 14"

15. **Rosalind Bloom**
Terra Incognita
Oil, collage, and sand on canvas, 26 x 60"

16. **Siobhan C. Brady**
Crime Scene II
Oil on canvas, 54 x 64"

17. **Joe Brenman**
Poet III
Stoneware, 17 x 10 x 15"

18. **Moe A. Brooker**
To be still & still moving
Mixed media on BFK paper,
42 x 60"

19. **James Brossy**
French Doors
Latex and cement on canvas,
81 x 55"

20. **Richard Buttari**
Crowd Scene with Minnie Mouse
Colored pencil on illustration board, 21 x 34"

21. **Lynne Campbell**
Dream (The Long Street)
Acrylic on canvas, 30 x 44"

22. **Philip J. Carroll**
Open
Oil on linen, 42 x 26"

23. **Giovanni Casadei**
Self-Portrait
Oil on canvas, 30 x 26"

24. **Richard S. Chew, Jr.**
Morning Sun, Manayunk
Oil on canvas, 30 x 40"

25. **Richard Ciocco**
No Smoking
Oil on canvas, 30 x 40"

26. **Nancy Citrino**
A Suitable Man
Monotype, 20 x 16"

27. **Beth Lea Clardy**
Exodus
Monoprint, 22 x 20"

28. **Mike Cockrill**
Independence Day
Oil on canvas, 64 x 90"
★ The Fellowship of the Pennsylvania Academy of the Fine Arts Award

29. **Patrick Connors**
Schuylkill River Bridge
Oil on linen, 48 x 60"
★ Honorable Mention

30. **Jacqueline Cotter**
Evergreen
Oil and mixed media on canvas, 40 x 40"
★ Purchase Award by the Fellowship Trust

31. **Kevin Cummins**
South 15th Street
Etching and aquatint, 6 x 9"

32. **Baily Bellenger Cypress**
Innocence Lost (A Memorial)
Mixed media (toy planes, plastic flowers),
120 x 84 x 48"
★ Mary Butler Memorial Award

33. **Fred Danziger**
Almost April
Acrylic on canvas, 62 x 74"

34. **Deborah Deichler**
A Man Looking Over His Shoulder
Oil on gessoed ragboard on panel, 13 5/8 x 9 7/8"

35. **Michael DeLuca**
Hand Tool
Oil on canvas, 34 x 40"

36. **Brian Dickerson**
Manayunk
Charcoal and graphite on
mounted paper, 7 1/4 x 8 1/4"

37. **Michael B. Doyle**
Still Life with Oil Can
Oil on masonite, 7 x 9"

38. **R. Elzo Dunn**
The Progress of Truth
Oil on canvas, 96 x 72"

39. **Ann Clardy Ekstrom**
Flora/Fauna Crackerjack
Oil on linen, 48 x 72"

40. **Richard Estell**
Cascadilla Bridge
Oil on panel, 40 x 48"

41. **Stephen Estock**
The Weight of Things Unsaid
Oil on linen, 48 1/4 x 36"

42. **Ingrid B. Faber**
The Pilgrimage II
Oil on canvas, 46 x 64"

43. **Jessie Fisher**
Rape of Satan's Daughter
Oil on canvas, 96 x 48"

44. **Steven Flom**
Belly in a Box
Limestone and poplar,
19 x 16 x 6"

45. **Renée P. Foulks**
Rites of Passage: Limbo
Oil on linen, 72 x 144"

46. **Carson Fox**
Jennifer II
Etching, 24 x 18"

47. **Larry Francis**
Rooftops
Oil on canvas, 36 1/2 x 86"

48. **Joy Friedman**
The Critical Eye — Louis B. Sloan
Oil on canvas, 15 x 13"

49. **Michael Gallagher**
Spiral
Oil on panel, 12 x 10"

50. **Margaretta Gilboy**
Wake Up Call
Oil on linen, 26 x 32"

51. **Barry Goldberg**
Toothsome
Oil and wax on linen,
55 x 33"
★ Pennsylvania Academy of the
Fine Arts/Fellowship Purchase
Prize and May Audubon Post
Memorial Award

52. **Barbara Goodstein**
Railroad Bridge
Modeling paste on painted
board, 22 x 22"

53. **Paul Gorka**
Swimming in Hell
Oil on canvas, 60 x 70"

54. **Peggy Gyulai**
Bartok: Concerto for Orchestra
Oil on canvas, 120 x 48"
★ Sandra Wolfe Karlin Memorial
Award

55. **Siegfried Halus**
Untitled
Photography — liquid light
emulsion and Polaroid transfer,
17 x 14"

56. **Raquel Montilla Higgins**
Bilingual Landscape #1
Pigment and ink on paper,
24 x 22"

57. **Ditta Baron Hoeber**
Rose Red, Rose White #22
B & W photograph, 3 1/2 x 5"
★ Riverbank Arts Award

58. **Christopher Hornbeck**
Untitled Hand 8
Soapstone, 10 x 19 x 9"

59. **Laura Hutton**
Specimen I
Copper, paper, glue, fabric,
thread, and Plexiglas,
20 x 18 x 10"

60. **Hei Myung C. Hyun**
Journey V
Acrylic on canvas, 48 x 36"

61. **Judith Silverman Jacobson**
Crisis
Oil on paper, 48 x 42"
★ Berthe M. Goldberg Memorial
Award

62. **Nancy M. Jaramillo**
Portrait of a Young Woman
Conté crayon on wood with
metal leaf, 17 x 13"
★ Honorable Mention

63. **Richard J. Johnson**
The Fifth Angel
Oil on panel, 48 x 48"

64. **Barbara Katus**
Hat with Brownie
Oil on canvas, 20 x 16"

65. **Mark Kaufman**
Poised
Woodcut, 16 x 12"

66. **Jeff Kellar**
Care
Wood, copper leaf, and glass,
16 x 22"
★ Purchase Award by the
Fellowship Trust

67. **Mee Jeong Kim**
Untitled
Oil on canvas, 60 x 50"
★ Honorable Mention

68. **Misung Kim**
Untitled
Foam, 96 x 72 x 48"

69. **Paul King**
Waiting Woman
Oil on panel, 30 x 24"
★ Jack Bookbinder Memorial
Award

70. **Tom King**
Rings, Lights & Haloes
Oil on canvas, 44 x 44"
★ Baker's Street Award

71. **John C. Kline**
Tornado Alley
Oil on canvas, 40 x 70"

72. **Rita Klinger**
Dancer II
Charcoal, 32 1/2 x 27"
★ Mabel Wilson Woodrow
Memorial Award

73. **Brian Kreydatus**
Self-Portrait with Scissors
Oil, 60 x 36"

74. **Clifford W. Lamoree**
Romantic View of Nuclear Power
Oil on linen, 36 x 48"

75. **Rodger LaPelle**
Black Spirit Vessel
Oil, 66 x 66"

76. **Victor Lasuchin**
I Have Dreamed That a Steep Ladder
Iris print, 46 x 34"

77. **Stephen C. Layne**
Untitled
Plaster, 11 x 6 1/2 x 7"
★ Leona Karp Braverman Memorial Award

78. **Victor Letonoff**
Model Sleeping
Oil on canvas, 47 x 56"
★ Mabel Wilson Woodrow Memorial Award

79. **Elaine M. Lisle**
Triple Play
Oil on canvas, 48 x 36"

80. **Patricia Hallock Lynn**
My Father Remembered
Gouache on Strathmore paper, 27 x 22"

81. **Douglas S. Martenson**
Starting to Draw
Oil, 46 x 78"

82. **Lydia Martin**
Scarlet and Stainless Steel
Oil on canvas, 24 x 8"

83. **Joanna Martinez**
Diptych—Moon Night
Acrylic and pastel on canvas, 64 x 75"
★ Honorable Mention

84. **Babette Martino**
The West Side of Conshohocken
Oil on canvas, 24 x 38"

85. **William R. Martone**
Winter Manayunk
Oil on linen, 28 x 34"

86. **Eric McDade**
Rose with Tape and Paint Smear
Oil on paper, 30 x 12"
★ Honorable Mention

87. **Sarah McEneaney**
Home
Egg tempera on wood, 30 x 40"

88. **Laurence McNamara**
Saltarello
Oil on wood, 13 x 11"

89. **David P. McShane**
Whitey
Acrylic on paper, 22 x 30"

90. **John T. Meehan III**
Stephanie and Clark
Oil on canvas, 12 x 16"

91. **Elizabeth Meyer**
Night Window II
Pastel on Twin Rocker paper, 30 x 22"
Courtesy of Northwestern Human Services

92. **Ellen Miller**
Dave 4
Oil on canvas, 28 x 20"

93. **Gregg Montgomery**
Figure/Landscape
Oil, ceramic, gold leaf, wood, and photography, 12 x 9"

94. **Jane Morren**
Baton
Oil on board, 29 x 10"

95. **Nobuaki Nakashima**
Kamishibai
Oil on canvas, 48 x 68"

96. **Elizabeth Osborne**
Blaze
Oil on birch panel, 38 x 48"

97. **Regina Overath**
Hoola Hoop Series II
Silkscreen on Plexiglas, 72 x 54"

98. **Katja Oxman**
An Open Window
3-color etching and aquatint, 24 x 24"

99. **Auseklis Ozols**
Good Morning America
Oil on canvas, 24 x 48"
Collection of Mr. and Mrs. James Coleman, Jr., New Orleans, La.

100. **Jamie Pearlstein**
Slippin'
Oil on canvas, 18 x 26"

101. **A. D. Peters**
Non-Renewable Resource
Assemblage, 66 x 66"

102. **Sarah Peters**
Horse and Rider
Bronze, 13 x 11 x 5"
★ Adolph Dioda Memorial Award

103. **Johanna M. Petropoulos**
Melancholia
Bronze, 11 1/2 x 30 x 20"

104. **Juan Puntes**
Kabuki Home
Cardboard, tape, and tacks, 22 x 20 x 18"

105. **Douglas W. Randall**
Mother Earth
Glass, 3 x 6 x 13"

106. **Jon S. Redmond**
Easy Target
Oil on canvas, 30 x 34"

107. **Huston Ripley**
Mourning Prayer
Acrylic on canvas, 78 x 96"

108. **Joan Roberts**
One
Mixed media, weathered plywood, and silver leaf, 78 3/8 x 30 3/16 x 2"

109. **Tony Rosati**
Day's End
Monotype, 8 x 6"

110. **Bruce Samuelson**
Untitled
Charcoal and pastel on ragboard, 40 x 32"

111. **R. David Schaaf**
August—Lansdowne Valley
Oil on canvas, 18 x 24"

112. **Richard Scheinfeld**
Untitled
Pastel, 30 x 22"

113. **Bill Schmidt**
Snare
Twigs, 15 x 7 x 6"

114. **Peter D. Schnore**
Walking Dunes
Oil on canvas, 23 x 30"

115. **Kathryn Schoepflin**
N & D Gin
Oil on masonite, 48 x 72"

116. **Wade Schuman**
Red Couch (Aftermath)
Oil on linen, 66 x 79"

117. **Scott Seebart**
Untitled
Oil on paper, 84 x 52"

118. **John Sevcik**
After Eden
Oil on linen, 14 x 30"

119. **David Shevlino**
Field of Corn
Oil on panel, 24 x 30"

120. **Jim Simmons**
Ultramarine Sky, Alamosa
Oil, 19 1/2 x 23 1/2"

121. **Joy Smith**
Ziggurat
Cast flax and metal,
20 x 10 x 10"

122. **Mary Spinelli**
Untitled
Alkyd on museum board,
26 3/4 x 34 1/4"

123. **William Stewart**
Self-Portrait
Oil on canvas, 52 x 40"

124. **Peter Stimeling**
The Little Artist
Watercolor, 27 x 33"

125. **Barbara Straussberg**
Moody Blues
Mixed media and acrylic on
canvas, 54 x 48"

126. **Rebecca Dvorin Strong**
Big Cloud
Oil on canvas, 16 x 12"

127. **Nancy H. Taplin**
Tipping the Scales
Oil on panel, 48 x 62"

128. **Robin Tedesco**
In Hiding
Oil on panel, 40 x 36"

129. **William G. Teodecki**
Purple is The One
Oil on canvas, 46 x 60"

130. **Glenn Thomas**
Cadiz
Acrylic on limewood panel,
39 1/2 x 51 3/4 x 2 1/2"

131. **John R. Thornton**
Too Late Now
Oil on canvas, 34 x 54"

132. **Mayumi Tomii**
Young Girl
Painted cherry,
19 1/2 x 9 1/2 x 17"

133. **Susan Ullmann**
Indigo Heights
Oil on paper, 29 3/4 x 22"

134. **Mark Wallison**
The Meeting
Pastel on paper, 26 x 33"

135. **Ronald Lee Washington**
Hide & Go Seek
Oil on canvas, 42 x 32"

136. **Gary Weisman**
Without
Bronze, 23 x 5 x 5"

137. **Steven Weiss**
*Our only Assurance of
Immortality*
Bronze, 42 x 32 x 20"

138. **Scott Wheelock**
The Air
Bronze, 60 x 12 x 12"

139. **Richard L. Whitehead**
*Straight Lines and Faces are
Illusory*
Sumi ink on silk, 14 x 17"

140. **Scott A. Williams**
Heave
Encaustic on canvas,
66 x 55"

141. **Elizabeth Wilson**
Scrabble
Oil on linen, 72 x 50"

142. **Harriet Zeitlin**
Terminal Illness
Acrylic on canvas, 54 x 216"

143. **Ruth Ziccardi**
The Last Supper
Oil, 60 x 54"

144. **Ted Zourntos**
Untitled
Oil on canvas, 84 x 67"
★ Award of Merit for an M.F.A.
student

SPECIAL AWARDS

The Percy M. Owens Memorial Award

Sam Maitin
Dulcifier I
Dimensional collage, watercolor,
acrylic, paper, and wood on
canvas, 36" diameter

Lifetime Artistic Achievement Award

Ben Kamihira
Two Women
Watercolor with Chinese White,
19 x 20"
Collection of Harriet Kravitz

Semi-Nude
Oil on canvas, 72 x 72"
Collection of Dr. and Mrs.
Chalmers E. Cornelius III

NON-JURIED WORKS
(In Memoriam)

1. **Thomas W. Golding** (1926–1996)
Teapot with Flowers
Acrylic, 11 x 14"
Collection of Nancy Golding

2. **Charles W. Hargens, Jr.**
(1893–1997)
The Lamplighter
Oil on canvas, 32 x 25"
Collection of Charles Hargens III

3. **Cranston Oliver Walker**
(1947–1996)
Enchanted Gate
Mixed media collage, 72 x 24"
Collection of Mr. and Mrs. Walker

4. **Ben Wolf** (1914–1996)
Self-Portrait
Oil on canvas, 20 x 16"
Collection of Ruth Wolf